THE FACE FINDER

THE FACE FINDER

Carol F. Fantelli

Carol Fantelli

MARBLEHEAD PUBLISHING ∾ RALEIGH, NORTH CAROLINA

Published by
Marblehead Publishing
3026 Churchill Road
Raleigh, North Carolina 27607

Cover illustration by Jesse Reisch

ISBN: 0-943335-07-8
Library of Congress Catalog Card Number: 97-73784

Printed in the United States of America

For Mom and Dad

Acknowledgments

I would like to thank my husband, Steve Murray, who believes in me and whose love is my strength. To my son who is and always has been my joy and inspiration. My sister Laura who encouraged me to keep sending more chapters, and my brother Dr. Floyd Fantelli for his invaluable forensic pathology expertise; Paul, LeeAnn and the rest of my family for their encouragement. To Susan and Kaye for pointing me in the right direction and keeping me on track. Pam Upton for her outstanding editing. Bonny Harrison whose literary "nuts and bolts" built my story. Mardie Meany for her sharp attention to detail. Margaret Maron, Brenda Jernigan, Harriet Hill, Ellyn Bache and Greg Lewbart for their positive reinforcement. Syd who never doubted it could happen. Stanley for the use of his name. Deb, Jane, Barb, Jan, Linda, Suzette, Massie, all the women of my GNO group and all my friends, who have been so supportive. Rachel Davies for sharing her expertise and solid advice. Dr. Page Hudson and Dr. John Butts for granting me permission to experiment with this technique in their lab. North Carolina Writer's Network for their valuable resources; Carolina Crime Writer's for the opportunity to share what I do. Dr. Billy Oliver, Rhonda Tyson, Cary Crane, and the North Carolina History Museum for the opportunity of a lifetime. Dr. David Weaver, for his anthropological expertise. Jesse Reisch for her exquisite artwork.

And especially, to my parents, who quietly instilled in us that there was nothing we couldn't accomplish.

PROLOGUE

*G*ravity seems innocent enough, unless it is pulling you to your death. Only then do you realize the power of this invisible force. I never thought much about it until now, as I fall headlong into its unrelenting grip, unable to reverse my direction. I have always believed few things on this earth are truly nonnegotiable. It is now my opinion that gravity has secured first place on that list.

I am shocked, of course, to be falling hopelessly to my death. But strangely enough, I am even more shocked by the abstract thoughts that pass through my mind as I grab and scratch at the air in a futile attempt to save my life. The seconds pass in slow motion, just as I had always heard from others who had a near-death experience and lived to tell about it. I don't expect I will be as lucky.

There is no life review, no angelic revelation, no mystical epiphany of any sort—just random thoughts. I am aware of the air separating the hairs on my head and pressing my clothes up against my skin, and I regret not having that second piece of chocolate cake. I think I should evaluate whether my life has been a success or a failure, or whether I could have been a better human being. But I don't. I don't even say a prayer for myself or anyone else. Instead I pray that I will land face up so that I might still be identifiable after impact. Am I afraid? Yes. But it is not death I fear; rather I am terrified by the possibility that I might survive and finish out my time in some mutilated rendition of living. I hope this will just be the end. And, although this was totally unexpected, I guess I am ready. Yes— I am willing now to surrender to gravity's hunger. In only a moment or so, the ground will devour my body, swallow my secrets, and digest my sins.

THE NORTH CAROLINA COAST

~

1990

$\sim$

$\mathcal{A}$ small crowd had gathered at the end of the pier. There was a hum of excitement, and even the employees who worked at Bo's Bait Shop had wandered out to take a gander. It was well known that some of the area's largest fish were caught right off that pier in the fertile but notoriously treacherous coastal waters of North Carolina. The proof was pinned up on the back wall of Bo's, where a hundred or more photographs showed proud-faced fishermen displaying their catch. And by all indications of the steadily increasing crowd gathered under the noon-day sun, yet another "big one" had been brought in today. Bo looked out the salt-crusted screen door that led to the pier and saw a reporter taking notes for the local newspaper. He had better clear a spot on the wall for a new photo.

About a quarter of a mile down the strand, a few Lighthouse Preservation Society volunteers decided to take a break from their work removing litter from the dunes around the lighthouse and walk down to the pier to see what the commotion was. As they approached the crowd, a photographer pushed by and ran up onto the pier. A bulging gray camera bag with broken zippers slipped off his shoulder as he fumbled inside it to find the right lens. He appeared anxious and sweaty but remained focused on his assignment. The youngest of the three volunteers, a college student, was immediately caught up in the excitement and followed the photographer to get a first-hand look. The other two volunteers, both retirees, stayed at the shore end of the pier, content to cool their feet on the weathered, ash-colored planks shaded by Bo's roof, and waited for the gossip to come to them.

$\sim$

"Hey man, can you see what they caught?" a surfer asked the old sun-dried fisherman standing next to him.

"Naww. Can't get close enough. I reckon it's a tarpon or kingfish. We'll see when they hoist it up."

The young volunteer moved past the surfer and nudged closer and closer to the photographer until he was literally on his heels. They were still quite a distance from the center of action and continued moving forward, with the photographer ignoring his shadow. A robust, red-faced woman, dressed in a bright orange-and-green flowered sun-dress that stuck in between the folds of her belly, suddenly turned around and bolted through the crowd, leaving ample room for both young men to step forward. There hadn't been this much excitement at the pier all summer. They were almost within viewing range now, and the volunteer caught a glimpse of something but couldn't make out what it was. If they could just move a little more to the right . . .

"Excuse me, please, Press—coming through," said the photographer, as if he read the volunteer's mind, and parted the onlookers with affected authority. Several people turned toward the man with the camera and then obediently moved aside. Never missing a beat, the volunteer moved right with him. The closer they got to the prize, the tighter and quieter the crowd became. Perhaps this was some sort of pier etiquette, like the silence around the greens at pro golf tournaments.

With skilled determination the photographer inched his way through the remaining layers of tightly packed people until he was so close to the catch that he was standing almost directly over it. The volunteer eagerly followed. It was a decision he would regret.

～

I

~

DEVON

~

1990

$\mathscr{S}$he could hear the phone ringing from the bottom of the stairs. It was always a race to see whether she could make it up the steps, unlock the swollen wooden door, and catch the phone in time. Usually it was some magazine sales campaign or someone taking a survey on something or other. In any case, it had become a game. She was almost at the top when she noticed she was doing it again. Counting the steps. Lately, no matter where she went, no matter how fast or slowly she ascended, she had resumed her old habit of counting the steps. *Twenty two, twenty three, twenty. . .*

"Dammit—quit doing that," she puffed out loud as she jammed the key in the lock, shoved the door open with her hip, and slammed it behind her. The phone was on its last ring when she all but leaped in the air to grab it before it quit.

"Hello?" she sputtered.

"Good afternoon, ma'am. I'm trying to reach Miss Devon Gardiner," said a crisp voice.

"Speaking." *Ma'am? Ugh.*

"This is Detective Whyte with the State Bureau of Investigation. Is it possible for you to meet me in my office tomorrow morning? There is something we'd like to talk with you about." She sensed that he was just being polite and that this was not really a request.

"SBI? Are you sure you have the right person, sir?" He didn't answer her. "Uh, tomorrow morning? Sure, I guess. Is 9:30 okay?" she heard herself say as she scribbled down the address.

"Yes, that will be fine, Miss Gardiner. See you then. "

*D*evon stared into the mirror as she brushed her teeth, wondering why she never even asked what this meeting was about. She racked her brain thinking of how she might have broken the law, but came up with nothing. It must have been something she did unknowingly. If that was the case, she rationalized, then why was she afraid to ask what it was about? The same reason as always. To avoid confrontation. Her automatic assumption of guilt made her an exemplary Catholic but a very insecure person.

It was 8:45 and she had just enough time to get downtown if she skipped her coffee. She put a call in to the museum and left a message for Nathan Richardson, her boss, that she wasn't feeling well and would be late. Her face flushed as she tried to sound convincing on the answering machine. She had never lied to Nathan before. There was no reason to. He was usually very good about letting her take a little time here and there when she needed it, and she was careful not to abuse his generosity.

It was amazing, though, how guilty one little phone call from the police had made her feel. She admitted that she had a tendency to "make" parking spaces for herself once in a while. But she did that only when she was in a hurry and absolutely couldn't find a space. Surely the police had more to do than to harass people for creative parking. Anyway, she had never gotten a ticket for it.

There were plenty of spaces available now as she pulled into the parking lot. Thirteen, fourteen, fifteen steps up to the double doors of the old Georgian-style building that housed the North Carolina State Bureau of Investigation. She was familiar with the red brick building as she was with most of the other architectural landmarks in downtown Raleigh.

Devon and her family had first moved to North Carolina from Ohio when she was twelve years old. Her father, who had lost his business to a regional competitor in the appliance repair industry, decided to move the family to an area where there were still growth opportunities for small businesses. "I just know this is going to be my chance to finally get ahead. There's a lot of promise in that part of the country." he said. "This is our opportunity to live the good life. It just might take a little more time, that's all." In her heart Devon knew that life was as good as it was going to get, but she pretended to share her father's enthusiasm and squelched her own dreams of a big house, fancy clothes, and traveling the world. The reality was that after the expense of moving and setting up a new business, they were barely able to afford a small bungalow on the outskirts of Raleigh in the tiny community of Willow Woods. There was enough money for them to get by on, but next to none left over for family entertainment. So on Sunday afternoons, Devon's family piled into the car and embarked on sightseeing tours of the capital city. It didn't cost much to drive around and admire the grand Victorian houses in historic Oakwood, or to walk the cobblestone streets of the old city market. They would sit and eat their ice-cream cones on magnolia-shaded city park benches and admire the fragrant blossoms hanging overhead. Other times they visited the museums that were all within walking distance of Capital Square and the Governor's mansion. In no time at all, Devon knew the streets and landmarks of Raleigh as well as she knew her way around a *Monopoly* board. These were memorable family outings that Devon looked forward to and cherished. Her father promised that once he got back on his feet financially they would take a trip to the beach or maybe buy a new color television. But it wasn't until Devon was grown up and working full-time that she took her first trip to the beach. And her father never did buy that new TV.

The receptionist directed her to Detective Whyte's office and she glanced at her watch to see that she was on time. He was on the phone and motioned her to have a seat. She smiled politely and sat down on one of two mud-brown faux leather chairs that were perfectly centered in front of his desk. She noticed that the seat cushions were dull and sagged in the middle and wondered how many criminals it took to wear out a chair. Her hands were sweaty and her mouth was dry. This was ridiculous. The only other time she had felt this nervous was in high school when Sister Laura Louise called her to the principal's office and wrongly accused her and three other girls of smoking pot in the bathroom. It was humiliating. She was such a good Catholic girl that she wouldn't even let Alex Rafhem French kiss her after the spring prom. The nuns warned the girls that in the spring the "sap rose" and boys were easily excited. She believed. So it wasn't very likely that she would smoke pot and risk ruining her reputation that way. Devon was brought up to do the right thing. And that's what she always did. At least that's what she told herself.

"Miss Gardiner, thank you for coming in," the detective said as he reached out his hand and offered a firm but nonthreatening handshake.

"Nice to meet you. Is everything okay? Look, if this is about the parking, I'm really sorry. I can pay the fine and I won't do it anymore. Will this go on my record?"

"Miss Gardiner, I don't know anything about your parking. We're interested in your work as a forensic sculptor. I understand you work for the museum and that you can use actual human skulls to re-create the faces out of clay?"

"Oh. . . yes. I've been doing it for about five years," she said. She was confused and a little irritated that she had skipped her coffee for what appeared to be a friendly little chit-chat. Why couldn't he have just asked her about this over the phone? "What exactly is it that you want to know?" she asked, hoping that she successfully masked the edge in her voice.

Detective Whyte got up from his chair, moved around his desk and casually leaned on one of three standard gray file cabinets. He was taller than she had thought and very neatly dressed. In fact, his entire office was immaculate. Papers neatly stacked in numerous piles, telephone messages organized, one pen and one pencil lying side by side on his desk. No coffee mug filled with leaky ink pens for this man. Even his plants were watered and carefully trimmed of any dead leaves. Everything about him belied the stereotypical image of sloppy, unkempt policemen portrayed on TV. Such attention to detail. She imagined he solved all of his cases. Anyone would be hard-pressed to look into this man's steely blue eyes and tell a lie. His features were not particularly intimidating, but there was an intensity about the way he looked directly into . . . no, through . . . her eyes that demanded nothing less than the truth. At that moment a wave of relief washed over her that her reason for being there was only to discuss her work at the museum.

"We would like you to help us identify someone," he began. "It's an interesting case. The victim died roughly forty years ago and the remains are in pretty good condition, considering how long they've been buried. Unfortunately, there weren't many clues at the scene as to who he was. There was some very expensive jewelry left behind: onyx cuff links, a diamond wedding band, and an eighteen-karat-gold pocket watch with the initials E-J-something, just lying there in the dust with the rest of his bones. But that's all we have right now to go on. So far, the cause of death indicates no foul play so we're guessing suicide, even though there was no note." He straightened his tie and smoothed his hair and then continued. "The third initial was worn off the watch from opening and closing it, I guess. We'd really like to know who this guy was and what happened to him. I think you could help us." He paused long enough for Devon to realize what he was getting at.

"You mean you want me to reconstruct the face of a suicide victim?" she heard herself say in a voice that was at least an octave higher than usual.

"Exactly." He said with a serious look on his face. "We're willing to pay you, of course, for your time, and you would be doing the S.B.I. and this guy's family a great service—whoever they are." Norman Whyte straightened up, smoothed his crisp white shirt, and ran his fingers through his hair. He came around behind her, close enough for her to catch the slightest whiff of lime aftershave, and then sat back down at his desk. He folded his hands and patiently waited for her answer.

"Oh . . . I don't think so," she began, but she was interrupted when another detective tapped on the side of the office door which had been left ajar.

"Excuse me for just a moment, will you, Miss Gardiner?" Detective Whyte stepped outside his office, closed the glass partitioned door behind him, and talked to the man with his back turned toward her.

"Norm, I couldn't help overhear you tell that woman it was a suicide. Did you get some new info on the case?" asked Detective Barrow.

"No, no. She's the 'face finder' from the museum. The artist, remember? Nervous type. I figured if I told her it might be homicide she'd never help us and I really want to try this forensic sculpting thing. Now, let me get back in there. I think I've almost got her."

Devon was close enough to the door to hear a few words like

"museum," and "artist," to realize that she was the topic of their conversation. But when she heard the word "homicide," she felt her knees go weak, depsite the fact that she was sitting down.

"My apologies, Miss Gardiner." He sat back down as his desk.

"Well, as I was saying," she started again, "all my work at the museum has been in archaeological reconstructions. Indians, early settlers and such. Nothing so. . . so gruesome. To be honest, I just don't think I'd have the stomach for it. I'm flattered, but no thanks. Besides, my boss would never give me that much time off," she added quickly, thinking that sounded more professional than her limp excuse of a squeamish stomach.

"Actually, I've already spoken to your supervisor—Mr. Richardson, is it? He was very obliging. In fact, Nathan gave me your telephone number. He thought it would be great experience for you and generate good publicity for the museum. Said it was even okay if you worked at the museum's art studio in the evenings. That way it wouldn't take time away from your museum duties."

The blood drained from her face, and she felt that prickly sensation of getting caught with her hand in the cookie jar.

"You spoke with Nathan?" she gasped. God, she knew it was a bad idea to lie. Now she felt like an idiot. Nathan knew she wasn't sick, she was exactly where he expected her to be.

"Miss Gardiner? You okay?"

"Yes, yes, fine" she mumbled. "Look, I need to think about this. And I really need to get back to work right now. So, may I call you in a few days and let you know my decision?" She didn't dare look him in the eye because she already knew her answer was "no."

Never mind that budget cuts and declining revenues had wiped out all possibilities of this year's raise, which she had been counting on; she still couldn't accept. The whole thing was just too morbid.

"Great, then." Devon said and held out her hand for a good-bye shake. "I'll call you next week, Detective Whyte." *Liar.* She was never going to talk to him again. Devon had already turned, anxious to leave, when she heard him say knowingly, "And if I don't hear from you, I can always reach you at the museum."

Even though she had her back to him as she closed the door, she knew he was smiling.

$\sim$

*N*athan was waiting for her in her cubicle when she arrived at the N.C.Museum of History. She tried desperately to read the look on his face. Was he angry? Was he enjoying this moment of righteous indignation? Or was he just so disappointed in her that there was nothing left to say?

"G'morning. Feeling better?" he asked finally, as his face broke into a devilish grin. "Can I get you something—perhaps a bar of soap?" He winked at her.

"Look, Nathan, I'm so embarrassed. It's just that I've never been called by the police before and, well, I wasn't sure what was going on. Anyway, I'm really sorry."

"Forget about it. But I hope you know that you don't have to lie to me just because you think you have a problem. My door is always open," he said earnestly.

"Thanks, I'll remember that." She exhaled with relief and felt her cheeks fading from crimson back to their natural color. Although Devon truly appreciated his offer, she could never come to Nathan for advice.

"You're going to accept the project, aren't you?" Nathan asked with a certain amount of expectation. She had been staring into space momentarily and was yanked back to reality with the sound of his voice.

"Huh? Oh, I don't know yet. I'm going to think about it and let Detective Whyte know next week," she answered sheepishly. Her head was pounding and it was only 11:30 A.M. She couldn't wait for this day to end. All she needed was a few hours to herself to unwind and she'd be good as new. For the first time she actually looked forward to getting home to her shabby apartment.

"Well, remember what they say about opportunity—it only . . . ," Nathan chimed.

"Knocks once, I know," she said.

But this was one opportunity that was going to have to wear out its knuckles, because she wasn't about to open the door.

It was almost 7:00 P.M. by the time Devon turned the key at 418 Barcroft Avenue. Her legs felt like cement pylons as she dragged them up to number 2A. No race, no game, no counting tonight. She was about to lift her well-worn brown loafer over the threshold when apartment 2B's door opened slowly and Milly's smiling face asked gently, "Working late again?"

"Not really," said Devon, "just a very long day. How are ya, Mil?"

"I'm good. But you sure look stressed. How 'bout a cup of Earl Grey and some dinner? I made enough for an army and besides, I'd love the company."

Devon was not really in the mood. She was tired and just wanted a bath, a bowl of cereal, and bed. But she couldn't say no to Milly.

"Sure, sounds great. Give me five to wash up and I'll be right over," she responded, wondering if she ever told the truth anymore.

~

The fragrance of the Earl Grey tea met her at the door of 2B and led her through the cozy living room to the kitchen, where Milly was waiting for her. The apartment was filled with large, overstuffed antique furniture that made Milly appear even smaller than her 4'10" frame. Nothing matched, and yet everything went together. Burgundy, gold, and deep green floral patterns covered the sofa. A favorite reading chair was draped with a hand-knitted shawl. The coffee table displayed numerous books on spirituality, philosophy, and ancient civilizations. There were candles and little folk art fetishes and a few cookie crumbs next to her bone china teacup, left over from afternoon tea. Milly was well read and well educated, from what Devon could tell. She never spoke of her past, saying it was irrelevant to the present or the future. Because her attitude toward her personal history was so nonchalant, Devon never felt the need to ask about it. Occasionally, Milly gave her opinion, but never advice, and the former only when asked. Milly was a mystery. A joyful, kind, and profound human being whom Devon loved and trusted more than anyone on this earth.

"So, what's going on?" Milly asked as she set down two cups on the small round kitchen table.

Devon found it hard to confide in anyone except Milly. When she was growing up, all the girls she knew were giggly, planned overnight parties, and talked endlessly on the phone. Sometimes they whispered things about her, but Devon shrugged them off and told herself it didn't matter, because she knew she was smarter than they would ever be. She never really had a best friend, just the friends who told her things in her dreams. Sometimes she wasn't even asleep when she dreamed. From the time she was very young,

Devon had always felt different from everyone else. Different in a way that made her feel odd and at the same time special. She had secrets about herself and about things that had happened to her that she could not share with anyone until she met her neighbor, Milly, a tiny woman with the most engaging manner. When Milly spoke, her voice was soft and melodic and her eyes never looked away from you. It seemed to Devon that she had known Milly forever. She liked that feeling.

Devon recounted the day's events as they sipped their tea. It felt so good to "confess." She told her friend about her little white lies and how bad she felt about it. Still she said, the SBI project would take up too much of her free time. Milly put her hand on Devon's, squeezed affectionately, and said, "Don't be so hard on yourself— give yourself a break once in a while. Now, give me the real reason why you don't want to take the project. You're always telling me how humdrum your life is. Here's your chance for a little excitement—an adventure. Besides, I know you could use the money."

How did she always know? "You're right, the museum reconstructions have been infrequent this year and I've been getting bored setting up displays and sculpting figurines. This project would be a real challenge, wouldn't it? And Lord knows, I could definitely use the money, but . . ."

"But what?" asked Milly. "It sounds so intriguing."

Devon looked out the small window, fiddled with the lacy curtains, and answered reluctantly, "I'm worried that I might, you know, "dream" while I'm working on it. And it being a suicide and all, I guess I'm a little scared."

The diminutive woman crinkled her eyes and replied softly, "I see."

Devon remembered the first time she told Milly about her dreams.

It was about five years ago, not long after she had moved in, that Milly invited her to afternoon tea for the first time. It became a ritual that they now indulged in every Sunday. She had accepted that first invitation out of politeness and wound up talking with her new neighbor until after dark. They laughed about what magpies they were. Truth be told, it was Devon who did all the chattering. It was the first time in her life that she had felt so completely comfortable being herself. They talked about her childhood, her family, her artistic talent, and eventually, her dreams. Milly wasn't suprised when Devon explained how sometimes when she touched objects she would have a split-second vision. These were what she called waking dreams.

On her way home from school in fourth grade, Devon found a rabbit's foot keychain on the sidewalk. It was white and gray and looked very soft. When she picked it up and held it in her hand, she saw the face of a young boy whom she thought she recognized from school but did not know by name. He was crying and looked very upset. She wanted to keep the keychain more than anything in the world, but the next day she took it to school, introduced herself to the red-haired boy, and handed him his lost rabbit's foot. He was both dumbfounded and pleased, and Devon walked away with a deep sense of satisfaction.

Occasionally, the dream visions were frightening, and sometimes sounds came into her head that no one else could hear.

One brisk October night after a high school football game, Devon went upstairs to her room to get ready for bed. She kissed her mother goodnight and patted her father affectionately on the top of his head as she walked by. Devon's parents didn't understand her at all, but she was a good-natured girl who followed their rules, and so they loved her in spite of her quirkiness. She bounded into her tiny bedroom and tripped over her school uniform crumpled on the floor.

She vowed to burn it after graduation. All her other clothes were put away or folded on top of the rickety dresser that was crammed into the corner. At least she didn't have to share it with her sassy little sister, Leora. Her bed was positioned so that when she lay on her back she could look out the window through the heavy oak tree branches and get lost in the night sky. It was the last thing she did every night before she closed her eyes. Until she met Milly, she had told all her deepest secrets to the stars.

That Friday night seemed like every other football Friday. Nothing special, nothing unusual. Devon crawled into bed and nestled under her blankets. She took one last peek out the window and drifted into a sound sleep. About 2:30 A.M. Devon awoke with a start. She had heard someone call out her name as clearly as if the speaker were standing at the foot of her bed. Her heart was pounding so hard she could feel it in her fingertips. It was a woman's voice—someone she knew—her Aunt Lydia. A few minutes later the phone on her nightstand rang, and when Devon answered, it was her Uncle William calling from St. Anne's Hospital. In a shaky voice he asked to speak to her mother, immediately. At precisely 2:32 A.M. Aunt Lydia, had been pronounced dead from a massive heart attack. Devon lay and stared at the ceiling until morning, wondering why her aunt had chosen her. She never told a soul what happened that night, but from then on she had a strong maternal feeling toward her Uncle William and little cousin Pauly and would call on them from time to time to see how they were getting along.

Devon sat across from her sandy-haired friend and hoped Milly would tell her what to do—but she knew, of course, that would be unlikely.

"Do you think I'm nuts for not taking this opportunity? What should I do?"

"Well, it's not for me to decide whether you should take the project. But I can imagine the family of this man would be mighty grateful to finally lay him to rest after all these years." There was a hint of empathy in Milly's voice, and then she continued. "Fear is probably the worst reason not to take this case, and the best opportunity for you to overcome your tendency to play it safe. Besides, even if you had a waking dream, what's the worst that could happen? It might be unpleasant or sad, or I suppose, even a little frightening—but it can't hurt you. It's just an intuitive flash of information from someone else's life. You see what I mean?" Her hazel eyes searched Devon's face for acknowledgment.

Devon got up from the table, helped herself to another miniscoop of linguine, and decided Milly was right. Milly was always right. She was sick of being a wimp. She had in front of her a chance to try something new, challenging, and even get paid for it. "I guess so. Besides, I haven't had any dreams since last year when I worked on the Piedmont burial ground project."

She remembered that project so well. Nathan had been all excited about the monies allocated for the new women's exhibit at the Museum of History. She would be reconstructing a face on a skull that was approximately four hundred years old. It was a young girl maybe sixteen to eighteen years old. Devon began the reconstruction like all the rest but had a feeling from the beginning that this small-boned Native American was someone very special. She handled the skeletal remains with particular care because of their delicate condition and also out of respect for the dead. As she placed her hands on the slightly elongated skull, she felt dizzy and took a sip of cola to clear her head. The second time she touched the skull, she felt dizzy again but kept her hands in place and moments later, to her surprise, experienced an overwhelming sense of peace. This gave way to a waking dream so vivid that Devon felt as if she were watching a movie in technicolor.

There was a young girl with many people gathered around her. She sat facing west with the amber glow of an autumn sunset on her face. The clan sat in a semicircle in front of her seeking her council. She was soft-spoken, and the tribal elders were listening to her every word. Despite her tender age it appeared she held a very important position in the village. She was a healer of sorts, a sage, blessed with knowledge beyond even her own understanding. And her beauty was admired almost as much as her wisdom. The girl's forehead was high and slightly sloped from ceremonial binding performed during infancy. Below that, deep-set, almond-shaped eyes rested above prominent cheekbones bronzed by the sun. Her full lips broke easily into a smile, and her hand movements were fluid and graceful. It was a pleasant dream for Devon as she watched and somehow sensed the feelings of these people and understood their ways. The reconstruction went quickly and smoothly because she had such a clear vision of who this girl was. Everyone marveled at the detail of her features, and Devon humbly accepted their compliments, though she didn't feel that all credit was due her. She had a great deal of help from the dream weavers.

Devon glanced up at the miniature cuckoo clock on Milly's wall and was surprised to see how late it was.

"Let me help you clean up real quick and then I've got to scoot. Thanks for dinner, Milly, and especially for listening." Suddenly Devon felt the weight of the day pressing upon every muscle and limb of her slender body.

"You're welcome, luv. And don't worry about cleaning up. I'll do it in the morning."

Devon was grateful for the reprieve and made her way to the

door. First thing tomorrow morning she would call Detective Norman Whyte and accept the project.

There was nothing worse than a fretful night of tossing and turning and she awoke as tired as when she went to bed eight hours earlier. She felt restless and anxious and connected it to her pending phone call to Detective Whyte rather than to the awful dream that vaulted her out of bed at 3:00 A.M. It was a dream about falling from somewhere into nowhere. Completely nonsensical. She wasn't even sure if it was she that was falling or someone else, but the sensation of tumbling through space out of control, was unnerving. It was the first time she ever had a dream like that.

Devon stretched and reached over to slam her alarm clock into silence. The dingy plaid comforter from her bed slid down onto the floor. Blindly she reached for it and made a half-hearted attempt to make up the bed. Her mother had given her that comforter as a gift when she went off to college, and she had been lugging it around ever since.

The Gardiners' meager income had made life difficult at times, and Devon always knew that if she wanted to attend college, she would somehow have to pay for it herself. And she did. She worked long hours for low pay at crummy little restaurants that hired students, and she accepted any student aid that she qualified for. Graduate school was an even greater financial challenge, but on graduation day Devon walked away with honors, which made it all worthwhile.

Leora would be graduating from high school next year, and Devon knew her parents wouldn't have the money for her college tuition, either. Her mother had never worked outside the home, and her father was nearing his retirement. She wished she could help, but a career in the arts rarely meant an excessive paycheck.

She fluffed her flat pillows and looked around the room. Maybe one day, when all her student loans were paid up and she was about ninety years old, she would be able to splurge and buy an entire ensemble for her bedroom. Something cheery and bright-colored with everything matching like the pictures of rooms in the home decorating magazines. The extra income from the police project might make that day come a little bit sooner. She sighed, brushed the hair off her face, and headed for the shower.

Devon was drying her auburn hair and thinking to herself that she wasn't too bad-looking for someone approaching her thirtieth birthday. Most of the beautiful women she admired in the fashion magazines or in the movies were very tall. Devon herself was 5'5" but always wrote down 5'7" on any registration form or application that asked for her height. It made her feel better and it was only a couple of inches, she rationalized.

Though she was by no means beautiful, her features were soft and her olive skin complemented her warm brown eyes. She had a definite sense of style that showed even in her low-budget wardrobe. People had always told her she was attractive, and if she didn't work so much maybe she would have more time to date. *Date whom?* Working down in the bowels of the museum didn't exactly expose her to the city's most eligible bachelors. She hadn't met anyone in years interesting enough to hold her attention for more than an hour. Most of the men she met just wanted to talk about themselves or sports, or to impress her with how sensitive they could be. For a while she endured the dating scene and then decided it was just more trouble than it was worth and never really very satisfying. She hadn't really given up—she just didn't put any effort into it any-more. And even if she did get involved with someone, sooner or later he would find out about her little "dreams" and take off faster than an eight-legged dog.

She slipped on her favorite navy slacks and a cable-knit sweater and went to the phone to call Detective Whyte. It was the right decision. He would be pleased to hear from her so soon, and especially pleased to hear she was accepting the project.

His card was down at the bottom of her purse and it took a few moments to find it.

"There you are," she said to the crumpled wad of paper under her lipstick case. She dialed his direct line. It rang twice before that same crisp voice answered. A wave of indecision washed over her momentarily when she heard his voice, and then disappeared.

"This is Detective Whyte. May I help you?"

"Good morning, sir. This is Devon Gardiner." Her confidence was back. She felt strong and very much in control.

"Devon, good to hear from you so soon," he said.

"Thanks. I called to give you my decision, as promised."

"Excellent. When do you want to get started?" he asked confidently.

Devon was more shocked than he was by what she said next. "I won't be doing the project. I'm sorry, I must decline. Good luck with it, though, and thanks again for the offer. Good-bye." And she hung up the phone.

There were little beads of sweat on her upper lip as she applied lipstick with a trembling hand. *What in the world was the matter with her?*

She grabbed her purse and an umbrella and hurried out the door. The last thing she wanted to do was be late for work a second day in a row or take the chance of running into Milly. She hoped Nathan would understand why she turned down the project, but how could he? She didn't understand it herself.

Her old blue Chevy was parked in her favorite spot. She was calmer now, and as she slipped into the driver's seat she was sure that she had done the right thing. There would be other opportunities for her to make some extra income. And if she really needed excitement in her life, she could take up rock climbing or something. Milly had made some valid points the night before, but Devon just did not want the stress of a police case. She was feeling much better about her last-minute decision and was going to put this whole thing behind her.

A stop at Donny's for a biscotti and cappuccino was first on her list, she thought with anticipation. Donny was everyone's favorite fair-haired Italian baker, a man whose robust appetite for fine food was surpassed only by his robust appetite for life itself. His was one of the few neighborhood shops that had so far been able to survive the continuous onslaught of mega-grocery store chains. Devon was one of his many fiercely loyal customers. It was good to get back to her routine.

Devon's apartment building did not have a parking lot, so those tenants with cars parked along the street. The rest, like Milly, who didn't own cars, rode the city buses. On this particular morning, Devon was pinned in by the cars in front and in back of hers. She would really have to be careful inching her way out. No problem, she had done it a million times before. The key was in the ignition and Devon was ready to roll. She could almost smell the coffee from Donny's just by thinking about it. She turned the key and her car started slowly. The engine hesitated, sputtered, and then began rocking and shaking. Finally it made an ungodly grinding sound and conked out. She tried in vain for about ten minutes to start it, but it was useless. The car was dead, and none of her special little talents could bring it back to life. Devon said a frantic prayer that it wouldn't cost too much to have repaired.

After she called the tow truck, she knew she had to face the inevitable. Call Nathan and tell him she would be late—again.

"Oh, not feeling well again?" he teased and then stopped when he heard the strain in her voice. "Just get here as soon as you can. I'll fill you in on our staff meeting at lunch."

Out her kitchen window, Devon caught a glimpse of the #29 bus rounding the corner of Greentree and Rowena avenues. She flew down the steps and raced up the street to the bus stop, reaching it just in time. As the bus lumbered down the city streets, Devon hoped and prayed that all she needed were new spark plugs.

"Telephone—for you, Devon, line two," announced her office mate, Dana. "Eddie's garage, I think."

"What? Oh my God, are you sure? Eleven hundred dollars?" she said into the telephone. "Isn't there some way you could fix it temporarily—you know, just until I can afford to do it right?"

Ironically, her prayer had been answered. According to Eddie, she did need new spark plugs—and a whole new engine to go with them. He had warned her over and over to check her oil level on a regular basis. There was a leak, he said, which would become serious if the oil ran too low. Eddie was right, and this was serious. She simply did not have the money to repair her car. Even if she saved all her "mad money" for six months, she couldn't begin to pay for it.

Dana gave her unsolicited advice about crooked car mechanics and offered her a ride home that evening. Devon accepted neither. She slumped down at her desk and stared at the wall. Tears welled up in her eyes and then overflowed. It seemed as though there was no way out of this one, and it was her own fault. She reached in her purse, which she had tossed on top of her desk, to find a tissue. Her fingers brushed over her wallet and circled around the crumpled business card with the name Norman Whyte on it. She stared at the card as though it were a huge chunk of Kryptonite and then slowly smoothed it out so she could read the numbers for the second time that day. There was no other choice. She picked up the telephone and dialed mechanically.

Detective Whyte was puzzled at her abrupt change of heart but nevertheless delighted to hear from her, and said so. Devon offered no explanation. She would begin working on the case immediately, and arrangements could be made to transfer the skull to the museum's art studio as soon as the paperwork was complete.

Eddie agreed to keep the car at the garage until she was ready to pay for it. The rest of the day passed in a blur. Dana and the other artists didn't understand why Devon was making such a big deal over her car and even chided her for being ungrateful for the unusual police project. They had no idea . . . 'unusual' was hardly the word for this project, and Devon's life was never to be the same again.

~

II

~

Mack

~

1950

*M*ack Landers opened a fresh pack of Lucky Strike cigarettes, struck a match, and took a long draw as he looked out over the Blue Ridge mountains. Although he had worked odd jobs all over the eastern seaboard, he had always wanted to see the mountains he was now seeing for the first time. Maybe this time things would be different. Maybe he would settle down here and finally get himself straightened out. His need to find a place that felt like home was still unfulfilled and left a dull ache in his gut. Any place other than the one where he grew up had possibilities.

Dorreen Landers insisted that her children call her by her first name rather than Mother, Mommy, Mom, or anything resembling that. Mack was a good child in a bad environment and most likely could have been a success had he been born into any other family. He was good natured and bright and was always trying to please his mother and win her affections. Dorreen's response, if there was one, was to reward him with a smartass remark. Motherhood was not something she took seriously, resenting the encumbrance it placed on her freewheeling and irresponsible lifestyle. She had part-time jobs that barely paid enough to put food on the table and pay the rent on their ramshackle trailer. The rest of her time she spent at the pool hall. She made sure, however, that there was always a little something left over for the real necessities—cigarettes and liquor. Her landlord was an ex-boyfriend who still had hopes of reforming Dorreen into a dutiful and docile housewife. When it was to her advantage, she played his game by promising him she would think about his marriage proposals. If the rent was really overdue, she would visit him late at night and not return to Mack and Bobby until morning. That would usually buy them some time until she could get the money together. One night during such a visit the old man collapsed of a heart attack and died. When the police arrived, Dorreen convinced them she was his common-law wife. She wasn't surprised that they believed her; she could be very persuasive. But she *was* completely surprised to learn a few weeks later that the fool had left her the trailer in his will. It was a dump, but it was free. And for a short while she seemed mildly content, but that didn't last long. Gradually she began to spend more and more time away and Mack and Bobby spent more and more time alone. Within the year, their mother had run off with one of her many faceless boyfriends, leaving no information as to her plans or whereabouts. The two boys were left on their own to survive.

Shortly after that both Mack and his younger brother quit school. Mack was barely fifteen and Bobby only nine. He tried to take care of his little brother as best he could, but Bobby starved for love, turned his emotions inward and was inconsolable. Mack tried to make things better but his efforts never brought him the results he was looking for—a pattern that seemed to follow him through life.

Neither brother had ever known their father, but they decided from their disparate facial features that it could not possibly have been the same man. Mack more or less adjusted to their mother's abandonment, but Bobby's emotional suffering ran deep, and eventually, as he grew up, it worked its way to the surface. He was drunk most of the time and barely supported himself by working at the local gas station. He was aimless and bitter, and he made no attempt to disguise his anger toward the world for dealing him such a rotten hand. Unlike Mack, he chose to stay in the coastal town of Buxton, living in the same wretched trailer that they had grown up in. He had no use for family or friends unless they had something that he needed. Sometimes Mack felt sorry for his brother. But it was useless. Whenever Mack tried to reach out to Bobby, the only thing he ever wanted was money. And that was something Mack never had enough of.

It was a long trip from the coast to the mountains, but Mack was feeling lucky from the moment he hitched his first ride. The last trucker who picked him up outside Winston-Salem took him all the way to the outskirts of Asheville. Said he had heard there were plenty of rich folk in that city who might need a handyman. Mack thanked him for the tip and wondered if his luck would hold out. He took one last drag on his cigarette and headed toward town on foot.

The ad in the paper said "part-time landscaper wanted." Mack didn't have a fancy degree, but he knew his way around a hedge or two. And he was even better at smooth-talking people into believing that he was exactly the man they were looking for—a trait he inherited from his mother. He was easygoing and friendly and started each new job with enthusiasm, sure he had finally found his niche. Then, after a couple of weeks, he would start gambling and eventually would have to leave town to escape his creditors. It was easy for Mack to get jobs—he just couldn't keep them. Unfortunately, the same held true for his relationships with women.

This time he felt more optimistic than usual. Maybe it was finally his turn to get a break. The chief groundskeeper was a short, stout man with a ruddy complexion and a receding hairline. His breathing was choppy and he spoke rapidly between breaths. He explained to Mack that the job was only for the summer and would end September 1st. Mack would be under his supervision and would be expected to perform routine landscaping tasks. The pay was low, but it included a bunk in the back room of the main greenhouse and three meals a day. That was as close to a normal life as Mack had ever hoped for, even if it was temporary. Mack assured the man that the job was perfect and that he was available to start immediately. If it worked out, maybe the little fat man would ask him to stay on permanently. It was a promising thought.

"Why don't you get settled in then, and tomorrow I'll show you the grounds and introduce you to the others. Dinner is at 7:30 P.M. in the servants' kitchen. And no smoking on the grounds. Welcome aboard, Mr. Landers." With that the boss turned and waddled off. Mack chuckled at the way his rump jiggled up and down and thought about how absurd he must look naked.

The following morning he was awakened at 6:00 sharp by someone shaking his shoulder frantically.

"Wake up, please, we are late. We are late," said a heavily accented voice.

"Yeah—what?. . . OK, OK . . . I'm up." Mack shot up from his cot and was totally disoriented for a moment. He had spent so many nights in fleabag rooming houses, shelters, and even on the streets that at first he thought the dark little face in front of him was a fellow drifter. However, when his vision cleared, he saw standing before him a clean-shaven, brown-skinned man in his sixties with a mixture of curiosity, panic, and friendliness all rolled up into one expression.

"I am Josè Rodriguez. We are working together. Hurry—the boss is no good when we are late," he said.

Mack smiled and threw on the clean uniform that Josè had brought for him. "Man, these rich people think of everything, huh, Josè?" he mused as he zipped up the last couple of inches.

As Josè scurried ahead, Mack noticed that his compact frame was in remarkably good shape for a man of his age. He wondered how

THE FACE FINDER   **35**

long Josè had worked for this family and guessed it to be the better portion of his life. He imagined how good it would be to have that kind of stability, and then at the same time wondered whether it would drive him crazy.

It took about two hours for the three of them to walk the grounds of the Winborne estate. The manor house was a four-story, thirty-two-room mansion with a fountain in front and the family crest mounted above solid oak doors at the front entrance. No wonder extra help was needed—the boxwoods alone would take a full-time position. The lawn was meticulously manicured around the circular driveway and continued down the stone path to the formal gardens. Josè informed Mack that he was only to mow the lawns and keep the hedges trimmed. A full-time gardener tended to the roses and myriad other flowers that were beginning to show off their springtime buds.

Mack was suprised that the little fat man had as much energy as he did. He walked along at a perky clip, pointing out the areas that needed attention. Despite the cool temperature of the spring morning, his face was almost purple, he was wheezing, and sweat dripped off his face. Another worker called him away to deal with a sprinkler problem, leaving Josè to impart the rest of his instructions. Just as well. Mack decided he disliked the way the "boss" looked down his nose at him and Josè. He was very familiar with that look, no matter how well someone tried to conceal it.

After lunch, Josè and Mack hiked back to the west end of the four hundred acre property. They had finished chopping down some overgrown brush from around the fence and sat down for a short break and a cool drink. Mack liked Josè and admired his tenacity. His leathery skin clung tightly to his sinewy body, and although he could not have weighed more than 140 pounds, he was rock-solid muscle. He worked nonstop and spoke only when spoken to. Mack guessed this man would take your secret to his grave if he was your friend.

"Want a cigarette?" Mack asked the dark-haired man.

"No smoking on the grounds . . ." Josè replied in a tentative tone.

"Aw, c'mon—you been eyeing my pack of Luckys since breakfast. We're out in the middle of goddamn nowhere—who's gonna know?" He held out the pack. "C'mon, have a smoke."

Josè stared at him for a minute, looked around, then grinned and accepted the cigarette. He inhaled with such ecstasy that Mack just handed him the whole pack.

"Keep 'em," he said. "I got plenty more." Somehow that small gesture touched Josè's heart and he opened up like the start gate at the race track. He started telling Mack about everything from Cassie the housekeeper's illegitimate baby to his treacherous border crossing from Mexico some thirty-odd years ago, when he left his wife and children behind in Chihuahua, Mexico, to find work in the U.S. He sent money home to them each month, but he had gone back to see them only twice in all those years. Josè missed his family more than anything, but he knew that as long as he worked for the Winbornes, his family would survive.

Mack had pegged him all right—as loyal as they come. It stung him to realize what a joke of a family he had come from. He didn't tell Josè much about Bobby or his mother—just that they had lost touch.

"Sounds like you got a real nice family, Josè. It's a damn shame you can't be with them. Maybe someday, huh?"

"Maybe. What about you?" Josè asked innocently.

"Naw—ain't met the right woman yet, I guess. But . . . someday I'd like to have some kids of my own. Spend time with 'em, take 'em fishin', bring 'em up right, ya know?"

"Well, you are a young man and I see in your eyes that you are good. God will bring the right woman to you when it is right. You must have faith, eh?" Josè was taking this whole conversation so seriously that now it was Mack whose heart was touched.

"Faith, huh? Well, okay, Josè. . . something tells me you know what you're talking about. I'll work on it." Mack smiled at Josè and gave him an affectionate slap on the back.

Each day Mack and Josè headed out after breakfast to start their duties. The little fat man rarely came around anymore, and it was obvious that he trusted Josè and found Mack's work to be acceptable. Mack was beginning to get really comfortable with the routine and found himself fantasizing that he might stay on another twenty-five years or so, like Josè. The paychecks were steady, and he was actually starting to accumulate some extra cash.

One Friday in the late afternoon, Josè and Mack were just finishing up the fountain hedges and gathering up their equipment when the front door opened and the most distinguished gentleman Mack had ever seen walked out. He was dressed in a gray pin-striped suit, silk tie, and Italian shoes polished to a mirror shine, and he was carrying a burgundy leather briefcase. His skin was smooth, every hair on his head in place, and he had clear sharp eyes. This, obviously, was the estate's owner, Mr. Winborne himself. The driver came around with the car, and Mr. Winborne started across the gravel driveway. Mack was mesmerized by the elegance and grace with which the man moved. It reminded him of the finest thoroughbreds at the track. Well groomed, well fed, and worth millions.

As Mr. Winborne came around the side of the car, Mack caught sight of a hedge trimmer lying on the ground, mistakenly left behind where they had been working. Mr.Winborne was looking in the other direction, telling the driver something, when his right foot caught the edge of the trimmer. He stumbled and began to fall awkwardly toward the ground. Mack lurched forward, grabbed his arm, and steadied him back to an upright position. It all happened so fast that the driver and Josè were left gawking and standing in the same positions as before. The briefcase flew into the air and landed about three feet away, but when Mack went to retrieve it, the man spoke abruptly.

"Thank you—I'll get that," he said in a gruff tone. He brushed off his suit, cleared his throat, and regained his composure. "Well, young man. I believe you just saved me from a nasty fall."

Mack was embarrassed but wasn't sure why. Perhaps because Winborne reminded him so acutely of everything he was not. And yet this sophisticated, blue-blooded aristocrat looked him straight in the eye without the slightest hint of condescension.

Suddenly, as if he had just waked up, Josè scurried over and began to speak rapidly. "Mr. Winborne—are you OK?" Josè's voice showed genuine concern.

"Of course. Now introduce me to this fine young man with lightning reflexes." Winborne smiled.

"This is Mack Landers—our new summer help," Josè said in his best English.

Mack started to put out his hand to offer a handshake but thought better of it. Just because he had kept the old man from taking a spill didn't exactly make them friends. Besides, when Winborne picked up his briefcase, Mack noticed how clean and well-manicured his hands were. His own hands were cracked and callused and his fingernails were caked with grit.

"Nice meetin' ya, sir," was all he could muster.

"Well, keep up the good work." And then, signaling the chauffeur to move aside, he slipped into the driver's seat of the car and drove away. That was the last Mack saw of him for two weeks. Until that afternoon, he had had no interest in his employer as long as his paychecks came in regularly. He had assumed Winborne was just another rich snob who drank champagne and counted his money all day. But now his paycheck had a face, made of flesh and blood just like him.

How was it that one man could end up in a mansion and another in a trailer when they were both made of the same stuff? That night he pumped Josè for information about his employer. They sat up late, smoking the forbidden Lucky Strikes and talking.

The Winborne family came from old money. Struck it rich during the California gold rush days and invested well. They never intended to stay in California, and after only a few years, packed up the family and made their way back east. New England was where they had their sights set on, but when they reached the Blue Ridge Mountains of North Carolina, they were so taken by the beauty of the area they made Asheville their home. It took four years for the mansion to be built and had been occupied by members of the Winborne family for the past one-hundred years.

Mr. Winborne was the last direct heir to the family fortune. He and his wife, Danielle, had had a stillborn daughter and a son, Garrett, who died during a flu epidemic when he was six. They tried unsuccessfully to have more children, and finally Danielle's grief drove her into a severe depression from which she never fully recovered. Winborne loved his wife deeply and tried everything to help her, but to no avail. Seven years later when she died—some say of a broken heart—he was distraught and locked himself in the mansion for two months. When he finally emerged he frequently could be heard weeping in the rose garden where his beloved Danielle had spent so many hours. Shortly after that, he began to take mysterious impromptu trips that lasted anywhere from a few days to a few months. No one ever knew where or when he was going. Nor did he say why he was leaving. On these peculiar trips, he drove the car himself and always returned looking contented and refreshed. The only items he carried with him were a small satchel of clothing and the burgundy briefcase. No one was ever allowed to touch the briefcase.

Occasionally there was gossip that he met a woman of the night, but no one really believed it. All of the servants cared for and respected Mr. Winborne. He was generous and kind and looked after them as though they were part of his family. The only thing he asked in return was honesty and a good day's work.

It was easy to understand Josè's loyalty to a man who promised him a job for the rest of his life. Once, one of the cooks lied to Winborne about a teapot that had been in the family for generations, and which she had accidentally dropped on the tile floor, shattering it. When he asked for his evening tea to be served in the heirloom teapot, she had lied and said it was missing. His temper raged, and the unfortunate woman was out the door before she could blink. Not because he so valued the tea pot, but because he had found the shards in the kitchen waste can and knew what had happened. Had she just told him she had dropped it, she might well have gone on to become chief cook. Winborne treated everyone equally and was as fair as anyone could possibly be.

Only the plump groundskeeper reminded the servants that they were servants. And he did that as often as he could. He was not in charge of all the employees by any means, but he relished what little power he had and used it to elevate himself to what he considered his station "above the others."

Mack was fascinated by the Winbornes' family history. How could anyone possibly know all their ancestors back as far as the 1850s?

He didn't even know his own father, let alone his grandparents, uncles, aunts, and other kin. He hoped that the fortuitous act of breaking Mr. Winborne's fall would put him in good standing for a permanent position come September. He would remind the little fat man of his good deed and implore him to pass it along to Winborne. He really wanted to be a part of this odd, tight-knit pseudo family. For now, it was better than no family at all.

He had only played the ponies and gambled a few times since he started the job and was feeling good about himself for the first time. If his luck held out, maybe he would have a chance at a happy life after all.

The summer flew by and Mack and Josè worked together like well-oiled machinery. They enjoyed each other's company and respected one another's differences. Mack learned a great deal from Josè's innate horticultural abilities and years of experience as a landscaper.

Toward the end of August, though, Mack knew his days were numbered. He had saved up most of his earnings and had done his best to please the little fat man. Josè wouldn't say one way or another what he thought Mack's chances were of securing a year-round position, but he did say that Mr. Winborne would agree if their "boss" recommended the position be extended. So in reality, if the fat man wanted him to stay, then he would stay. It was as simple as that.

Mack had a kind heart but it could turn to stone if it meant survival. He thought long and hard about the approach he should take with his boss. It was a gamble. If he kissed up to him, he might inflate the vain little man's ego enough to wield his power in Mack's favor. He would really like the idea that he had played such an important role in Mack's future. On the other hand, Mack knew the bloated little pig didn't really like him and, therefore, might take even greater pleasure in kicking him out on his ass. It was a tough call. Mack decided to play his aces and outwit the boss with cunning manipulation and blatant flattery. He figured he had nothing to lose and everything to gain if he was right. There were only three days left of his employment agreement. Tomorrow he would talk with the weasel and work his magic.

When he thought back to all the times he had talked his way in and out of tight situations, he laughed. What was he worried about? This was going to be easy. He was anxious for the morning to come so he could get this over with and make some plans for his new life. In a year or so, maybe he could even buy an old used car.

There was one last cigarette in the pack, and he reached to get it, then put it back down. "I'll save it for tomorrow and share it with Josè. We'll celebrate my new permanent position," he said aloud to himself.

Through the window, Mack could see his boss sitting at his desk. He had never really been inside the servants' quarters before. Every time they met it was at the greenhouse. Josè and Mack were the only two employees who shared the converted storage room in the greenhouse. That was where Josè stayed when he was first hired and he had been there ever since. Mack was used to make-do living arrangements, and both he and Josè liked the privacy. The servants' building had been a carriage house at one time before being remodeled to accommodate the live-in help. After his wife's death, Winborne had preferred to be alone in the main house at night and as much as possible during the day. The former servants' quarters on the fourth floor of the mansion remained empty. The housekeeper, maids, and cooks left every evening after dinner and returned again in the morning.

Mack tapped lightly on the window, and the little man looked up and waved a doughy hand for him to come in. Mack had showered, combed his hair carefully, and used a new razor blade for a good shave. His clean uniform was still slightly damp. As he entered the stuffy office, the man who held his future never looked up from his paperwork.

"What is it, Mr. Landers?"

"Well sir, I was wonderin' if I might have a few moments of your time," Mack said with what he imagined to be Sunday school manners.

"You've already had a few moments. Is there a problem?" the boss snapped.

"Absolutely not, sir. Ya see, that's just it. Workin' for you has been the best thing that's ever happened to me." So far, Mack was telling the truth. "And me and Josè, well, we get along about as good as two people could." Right again.

"What's your point?" he asked, putting down his pen.

"Well, I only got three more days till September 1st, and I was hoping that since you was so generous to hire me in the first place, and I learned so much workin' here for you, that maybe we could talk about me stayin' on, ya know, permanent." No reaction. Mack continued, " I know a man with your brains and expertise could get a good job anywhere he wanted. But somebody like me, well, it ain't so easy." He was listening. "And I never seen anyone who could trim up a hedge faster'n you. Even, too. So I know I still got a long ways to go to measure up to yer know-how, but I sure am willin' to work hard and learn. And I wouldn't ask for no pay increases, neither."

"Mr. Landers, the job was a part-time summer position only."

Mack had anticipated a little resistance. He was right on cue.

"Yes sir, yes sir, I know. But if I was to stay on during the year, well, you could take a little more time off. You been workin' real hard all them years, and hell, you deserve it. I could take up all your Saturday duties—I wouldn't mind one bit." Mack had his interest now.

"Hmmmm," was all the groundskeeper said.

"Look, just think about it, OK? I'll come back tomorrow and you can let me know. I just sure hope you'll give me a chance, sir." *Don't say any more, you got him where you want him.* As he stepped back from the desk to leave, the little man looked him up and down.

"Very well, I'll think about it, Mr. Landers. Good-day." And he returned to scribbling his paperwork.

Got him. He couldn't wait to smoke that cigarette with Josè.

He lay awake most of the night making big plans for his new life and tried to figure out how much he'd have to save each month to buy a car. He was going to get himself a fancy watch someday, too. Josè sat across from him and listened. As Mack was talking, he realized that Josè brought out the best in him. Josè made him feel respectable, capable, intelligent, and most important, hopeful. Josè was the first person in Mack's life that didn't consider him a loser, but merely a victim of what he called "bad economics." Mack wanted to believe in himself more than anything in the world and Josè made him feel that there was no reason not to. This was finally his break, he told Josè, tomorrow when his job was expanded to a full-time position he would be able to start his life over. When Mack asked him why he was so quiet, he replied that he believed it was bad luck to put the cart before the donkey. Mack let out a roar of laughter and slapped him on the back. "After tomorrow, Josè, all my troubles are over! You and me is gonna celebrate for real. I'm gonna cash my check and we're goin' to town for a restaurant meal and some beers. . . and maybe we'll stop in at Stubby's pool hall and rack 'em up a couple times. Hell—I'll even throw in a whole case of Lucky Strikes. You'd like that wouldn't you, amigo?" Mack asked excitedly.

Josè smiled at his friend and said simply, "That would be good."

In the morning, Mack mowed the lawns surrounding the tennis courts and trimmed the hollies near the poolside cabanas. It was almost lunchtime by then, and he decided it was the right time to go to the office and get his good news. When he arrived, the fat man was at his desk again, munching on apple cake and sipping tea. There were crumbs in the corners of his mouth, and after every sip he twitched his lips back and forth like a rodent. As soon as Mack laid eyes on his boss, intense feelings of resentment rose up inside him. He was aware that this man, like his mother and Bobby, brought out the worst in him. He squelched his feelings and reminded himself that everything he wanted could be his if he played it smart and kept his cool. Mack walked into the office with a smile on his face. "Good morning, sir. Ain't it a beautiful day?" he asked cheerily.

"Yes, I suppose so. Why don't you sit down."

Mack was eager to discuss the details of his new employment contract. He sat down and assumed the papers on the desk pertained to that very matter. His boss finished signing one last paper, slid it in front of him and said matter-of-factly, "Here is your final paycheck, Mr. Landers. You may take the rest of the afternoon to collect your personal belongings, and stay the night. In the morning I expect you to be on your way. Good-luck with your future plans." He continued to sip tea and scribble on his paperwork.

Mack was paralyzed. He saw the man's lips moving, but all the wrong words were coming out. *Last paycheck, be on your way, good luck with your future plans . . .*

What the hell was going on? His anger swelled up in his throat and his face felt hot, but he controlled himself. "But, I don't understand," he said. "Yesterday you said you'd think it over and . . ."

"And I did," the boss replied. " I just decided that Mr. Winborne doesn't need another full-time groundsman. Josè can handle the winter workload just fine. If you want to come back next summer, I'll give you first consideration. Now, if you don't mind, as you can see, I have quite a bit of work to catch up on." Then he looked down and began to write. Conversation over.

Mack crumpled his paycheck in his fist and stormed out of the office. He knew it was useless to try and persuade the little rat any further. He had lost the gamble, and if he looked at that pug face one minute longer he would be tempted to put his hands around the pudgy neck and squeeze the life out of him. Why couldn't things go his way—just once? As he walked across the lawns, one of the housemaids said good morning, but he never even looked at her. He got back to his quarters,ripped off his uniform, which he tossed on the floor, and put on his old clothes. His last cigarette was lying on Josè's bunk. He lit it, took a few puffs, and slammed out the greenhouse door. He had to get away from this place. Mack threw the butt on the ground defiantly and left it smoldering on the walkway as he headed for town.

~

Mack's fury pushed him from bar to bar and from pool hall to poker table until his entire paycheck and all but twenty dollars of his summer earnings had been gambled and drunk away. He had no recollection of how he made it back to the estate that night, but Josè was sitting on the end of his bunk when he awoke in the morning. He handed Mack a cup of hot coffee and told him he had heard from the others what had happened with the boss. Sympathetically, he said he wished there was something he could do.

"You been a good friend, Josè, and if my horse ever comes in, well, I won't forget ya." They shook hands, and Josè hurried on to start his daily duties.

Mack packed up his few belongings and took two aspirin for his headache. He still couldn't believe he was leaving. There had to be some way to keep this job.

"C'mon—think hard—there's got to be a way," he said aloud as he stuffed a pair of socks in his duffel bag. And then it hit him. Why didn't he think of this before? He splashed cold water on his face, combed his hair, and made a beeline for the manor house.

"Twenty bucks says old man Winborne will give me another chance," he bet himself. Of course he would; he liked Mack. He would understand and be flattered that Mack wanted to work for him so badly. As he approached the manor house, he saw that the car had been pulled around front and left with the motor running, waiting for Mr. Winborne. No driver. Mack glanced in the car and saw the familiar overnight satchel lying on the back seat. Old money bags was going on another mystery trip. Mack smiled. His luck was back. Even five minutes later and he might have missed him. Timing was everything.

The front doors were slightly ajar as Mack rapped the lion's head door knocker. He looked at the cracked face on his watch and realized it was only 6:40 A.M. The house staff had not yet arrived. The car was still running—Winborne would be out any second. He waited a few minutes longer, but still no sign of him. "Aw, what the hell," he muttered and pushed open the heavy door. It was like stepping into another world.

The entrance hall was huge, and overhead hung an enormous crystal chandelier. Mack stood there with his mouth gaping open, not sure what to do next. Since he had never been in the manor house before, he had no idea where to locate Mr. Winborne. Four rooms opened off the foyer, two in front of the staircase and two behind it. To his immediate left was a music room whose walls were covered from floor to ceiling with dark mahogany paneling that smelled of fresh linseed oil. A large, intricately designed rug on the floor was worn with age but still bespoke elegance. Along the back wall, were a harp and a small grouping of chairs covered in silky fabrics and an ornately carved table. And above the fireplace was a portrait of a woman with a young boy sitting in her lap. Mack guessed them to be Danielle and Garrett Winborne. In front of the latticed window was a baby grand piano with several small old-fashioned picture frames and a few silver candlesticks on the top of it. Scattered about on various side tables were more pictures of Winborne, Danielle, Garrett, and other members of the Winborne family.

To his right was another room almost identical to the first. This was a formal parlor. Another oriental rug, but newer than the other and in richer colors of deep blue and red. On the walls hung various oil paintings like those in museums. Probably passed down through the generations and worth millions. There were pedestal tables that displayed bronze sculptures and busts. In front of this fireplace was a narrow sofa barely big enough for two people, a wood inlaid table, and two pale green silk-covered chairs. Heavy purple velvet draperies almost blocked out the early morning light that was trying to creep into the room. And in one corner was a small table with a lamp made of hundreds of tiny pieces of colored glass and next to it some small figurines. Mack had never seen so much opulence.

He debated whether to look in the other two rooms but decided instead to move toward the winding double staircase in front of him. He was not at all comfortable and wished he had waited outside. The pink marble steps were polished to a high shine and looked as though they were covered with a thin sheet of ice. At the landing the stairs split and curved to either side, joining again on the second floor.

"Mr. Winborne, sir?" he called politely. He didn't want to piss the old man off. What if Winborne found him in his home and thought he was up to no good? He started to panic and had turned to slip back out the door when he thought he heard something. He listened again and sure enough, someone was upstairs. Mack started to take a step and saw Winborne dash out of the room at the top of the stairs and hurry down the hallway out of sight. Mack called out to the gentleman again, louder this time, but it was too late. Winborne didn't hear. *Well, I guess I could just go up there and wait for him. He's gotta' come back sooner or later and I ain't got nowhere else to go.*

He climbed the staircase and entered the room at the top. It was the office and library. A real man's office—leather sofas and chairs, windows with no draperies. The walls were lined with bookshelves filled to capacity. It smelled like stale cigar smoke and a lingering hint of men's cologne. Mack liked this room. He thought two men could really talk in a room like this. He sat down in one of the high-backed leather chairs in front of Mr. Winborne's desk. It was then he caught sight of the burgundy briefcase. Dead center on the desktop. Mack just sat there, staring at the case. He prayed Winborne would come in the room right then, and the temptation would be over. But he didn't. Everyone was dying to know what the secret of the briefcase was, Mack included. What was in it? Why was he so protective of it? And there it was like a prize on display at the state fair. All he had to do was lift it open. He checked the time on the grandfather clock. It was only 6:45. He had been in the house five minutes, but it seemed like an hour. In fifteen minutes the housekeeper and maids would arrive. If they found him in the house, they would make a terrible scene; he would definitely lose all hopes of keeping his job and probably get thrown in jail. Should he wait for the old man? Dare he look in the briefcase? He had to decide now. Still no sign of Winborne.

Ten to one he could look in the briefcase, close it back up, and still sneak out of the house before Winborne or the staff ever knew he was there. Bet's on. Last call. Mack sprang out of the chair, walked over to the desk and touched the briefcase. No harm in just looking. *Nice*, he thought. *Real smooth leather.* With one hand on either corner, he lifted the lid of the legendary case slowly, as if it were sacred. He kept his eyes on the door until the briefcase was opened completely. Still alone. When he looked down, he let out a whimper and felt his knees go weak. It was stacked top to bottom, side to side, with one-hundred-dollar silver certificates. His hands touched the neatly arranged bundles and he began to count them. Each bundle contained ten thousand dollars and there were twenty bundles. Two hundred thousand dollars total. Mack was dumbfounded. The only other item in the case was a plain letter-size white envelope rubber-banded to a few bundles in the middle of the briefcase.

"Sweet Jesus, no wonder the ol' boy never lets anybody near it," he whispered. "What in the world is he doing with all this? Where does he go on them trips that he needs that much money?" He shook his head in amazement. Oh well, what difference did it make? He certainly wasn't going to tell his secrets to Mack. And all Mack really wanted Mr. Winborne to tell him was that he could keep his measly job.

He sighed and then started to close the briefcase with one hand, holding it in place with the other, when he looked up and saw a man in a tweed jacket standing in the doorway of the library—with a shotgun pointed straight at Mack's head.

III

~

DEVON

~

1990

*T*en days after Devon accepted Detective Whyte's project, a plain brown box arrived from the medical examiner's office. It was hand delivered with "fragile" stickers pasted all over it. Devon knew immediately what its contents were. She signed for the package and carefully placed it on her work table. It took her two more days to muster up the courage to open it and take her first look at the skull. And even then, she examined it by observing as much as possible while it remained inside the box. She rationalized that there was no need to touch it until she was ready to start the sculpture. It was in remarkably good shape for being as old as it was. No teeth were missing, and there was no visible damage to the skull from either animals or the elements. It was common for small animals to bite, chew, or scratch skeletal remains, leaving tell-tale marks. Most important, the climate, soil condition, and moisture content of the environment where the bones were buried determined to a great extent the overall condition of the bones.

Alongside the skull was a report from the medical examiner with the usual information such as the deceased's age, weight, and race. According to the report, he was Caucasian, approximately fifty years old, average height, and average weight. He had been in excellent health at the time of death and apparently had died from head injuries. There was one bit of information about a "fractured C2" that she didn't understand but that was mentioned several times in the report and appeared to be of significance. The report continued on and on with medical details that were useless to Devon. But she read the whole analysis anyway, feeling it was her duty, and stopped at certain sections that were in plain English and easy to understand. For the most part it appeared that the deceased had led a healthy life with no severe childhood illnesses and only one injury worth noting:

The thickened right tibial shaft fragment has several possible causes. One possible cause is a healed tibial shaft fracture, with the thickened cortex being the result of normal processes of fracture repair. There is moderate porosity and moderate periosteal bone deposition on the shaft fragment, suggesting infection and skeletal response to the infection following the possible fracture. Radiographs of the shaft fragment do not show a previous fracture line but do show some evidence of bone callus that would have been involved in normal fracture repair. It is possible that the fracture healed with slight angulation or distortion of the bone and would have resulted in a minimal alteration in appearance and function of the leg. Another possible cause of the thickened tibial shaft cortical bone could have been a local bone infection. Local osteomyelitis can ensue from infection of the bone from adjacent soft tissue wounds, particularly in areas like the anterior tibial shaft, where the bone is covered only by skin and is not deeply embedded in muscle or other tissues. If the tibial shaft condition is due to osteomyelitis, the condition apparently had not spread to any other areas of the skeleton and may not have had particularly important consequences for the person.

The report was signed by Dr. James Florio. Devon jotted down a note to call Dr. Florio next week for an explanation of the C2 fracture and then get down to the business of finding a face for this poor soul. Then she would collect her check from Detective Whyte, hand it over to Eddie, and have her car and her life back in no time.

"Dr. Florio? This is Devon Gardiner from the museum."

"Hello Devon. I thought I might get a call from you. Please, call me James. How's the reconstruction going?" he asked.

"Well, I haven't really gotten started yet. I just had one question, if you don't mind." Devon wondered whether Florio's looks matched his pleasant manner.

"Of course. How can I help?"

"On page 3 of the postmortem report, the cause of death refers to a fractured C2. What is that?"

"Oh, a fractured C2 is a broken neck. Specifically, it refers to the location of the second vertebrae," he answered simply.

"And how would it affect the death?" Nice intelligent question, she thought. She was trying to think of more just so she could stay on the phone a little longer. Devon liked the relaxed cadence of Dr. Florio's voice. He sounded like a man who kept his cool even under the most stressful situations.

"Well, if the neck is broken at this location and the spinal cord is severed, which is what happened to this fella, then the brain is unable to communicate with the rest of the body's organs. The lungs quit breathing, the heart stops, and without immediate intervention, the victim is dead within, say, 5 to 6 minutes. The only blessing is there's no pain." He paused for a moment.

"I see." Devon swallowed hard and was a little sorry she asked. "What about the tibial fracture? Any importance to that?"

"I doubt that it gave our man much trouble. Maybe one leg a fraction shorter than the other. Any other questions I can clear up for you?"

"No, I guess not. Thanks for your help Dr. Fl . . . uh, James."

"No problem. Listen, give me a call again, anytime. I'm really interested in what you're doing and I'd like to see the reconstruction in progress. Would it bother you if I came down to the museum one evening to watch you work?"

He was so charming and she was so fascinated with his seemingly effortless conversational skills that she almost answered "yes" automatically. Until she remembered.

"Actually, I never let anyone watch while I'm working on a reconstruction." How could she explain this to him without sounding like a New Age nut case? "It's nothing personal," she continued, "I just can't concentrate if someone is watching." She hoped her explanation seemed plausible enough. After all, it was better than the truth. If she had a flash while he was standing there, he would think she was insane or having a seizure or something. But she really did want to meet him. "How 'bout this? Maybe after I've completed some of it, you could come by and I'll show it to you."

"Sounds great. Just say when. I'd invite you over to the coroner's office to see my work, but I don't think you'd enjoy it much," he laughed.

Devon pictured arms and legs strewn about casually on the tops of tables and desks. Ears and noses and maybe fingers lying on the window sills in between the plants. Did they put the parts back in the body when they were finished with the autopsy? Ugh. He was right—she wouldn't enjoy seeing his work.

"I suppose you're right," she replied with a weak laugh. "Well, thanks again. I'll be in touch."

"Good, and don't keep me in suspense too long. I can't wait to see this guy's face."

And I can't wait to see yours, she thought, and hung up the phone.

～

A week later, after procrastinating in every way she could possibly devise, Devon forced herself to return to the museum after dinner to get started on Detective Whyte's mystery man. The summer days had abruptly surrendered to an autumn chill, and the daylight hours were quickly evaporating. It was dark when she entered her security code into the box by the employees' back door entrance. This was the first time she had ever been in the museum alone after hours. When she worked overtime on special projects it was usually with a group of her co-workers. They would order in a pizza and everyone would walk out to the parking lot together when they were finished. Tonight was very different. Unlike the symphony of conversation, chamber music, and commotion that reigned during special evening events such as exhibit openings and lectures, the museum was quiet and peaceful. Almost holy. The security guards who roamed through the museum during the day had locked up and gone home at 5:00 P.M. like everyone else. Tonight she was alone.

Milly was concerned about her riding the city buses alone at night. But she reassured her friend that the bus stop in front of the museum was directly under a street light, and besides, she didn't anticipate being without a car for more than a week or two. Her footsteps echoed through the long corridors and as Devon approached the artists' work area, she shivered. She shrugged it off and reminded herself that once she got into the project she would be fine. She was good at this, and it was a chance to gain some significant recognition for herself in her field, boost her self-confidence, and show some gumption. In her mind it was easy to be strong. She flipped on the overhead lights, threw her purse down on the table, and walked toward the brown box with conviction. And although her hands were shaking a little, she reached to fold back the cardboard flaps. Abruptly she stopped and pulled her hands back.

Walkman. Brilliant idea. There was no reason on earth why she had to think about this person's demise while she was working on it. Dana always left her walkman in the bottom left drawer of her desk. Devon sprinted over to Dana's desk. She could pop in a tape, listen to some rock n' roll or jazz, and keep her mind completely occupied so that nothing unwanted could seep in. Bottom drawer. Bingo. Devon smiled and felt she was finally ready to tackle this project.

On Devon's work table were all the usual tools and materials for a facial reconstruction. Everything was lined up neatly, not unlike Detective Whyte's desk. Devon purchased a new notebook for her project journal. In it, daily entries were made on her progress, procedures, and observations. A chart with measurements for average facial tissue thicknesses was lying underneath several razor blades. Next to the measurement chart was another color diagram showing in complete detail the configuration of the facial muscles. A tube of duco cement, rubber eraser refills used for tissue depth markers, some cotton balls, prosthetic eye caps, numerous boxes of nonhardening sculptor's clay, and a small pair of surgical calipers all occupied places of importance. The procedure was always the same. She began by entering the date and name of the project in her journal with a brief outline of the nature of the project.

October 2, 1990   *Forensic Reconstruction/SBI Project*

Reconstruction of Caucasian male, age—early to mid fifties, general health very good. Average height approx. 5'11", weight approx. 170 lbs., medium build. Lower mandible intact and no teeth missing. Skull is in good condition. Nasal spine about 75% intact and in good condition for measurement. Cause of death, fracture of the second vertebrae and injury to first and third vertebrae. Possible suicide?

Next she took precise measurements of specific facial bones that determined the length, width and projection of the nose. The width, of the front six teeth determined the corners of the mouth. The color of the eyes was anybody's guess for Caucasians, so she chose a pair of hazel prosthetic eye caps for this case. There were never any clues to the size and shape of the ears because of the soft tissue decomposition after death. So for convenience she had several sets of nicely sculpted ears in small, medium, and large that she kept in a plastic box and used over and over again.

When Devon had first heard about this type of sculpture, she was in grad school. She had seen the movie _Gorky Park_ and was fascinated by the whole process of putting a face back on a skull. Sculpture was always her favorite area of study in art school and she was convinced she could do it. She gathered as much information as possible from the library and was amazed to learn that the procedure had first been done successfully in Europe as early as 1883. A Russian paleontologist named Gerasimov introduced the technique to criminologists in 1939. The problem was it was a technique seldom used and she could find no university, art school, or instructor who knew how to complete a forensic facial reconstruction.

Out of desperation, she contacted the FBI and struck gold with a young agent who was familiar with the technique. He told her that it was really a last resort when all other efforts at identification were exhausted. There were so many other ways to determine someone's identity that it was rarely used. Dental records were common and so successful at establishing identities that they precluded such alternative methods as facial reconstruction. The agent knew only one artist doing this type of work; he gave Devon the name of a woman in Texas he had read about. It was one of the few times in her life Devon took a chance and pursued something that had neither a definitive nor promising outcome. The woman, when contacted by telephone, confirmed what the agent had said about no training programs being available. However, she had made an educational videotape of the procedure for law enforcement officers and told Devon she was welcome to borrow it for three days if she wanted to. Devon did. For those three days she watched the tape over and over, taking notes, and then sent it back. That was all the formal training she had the luxury of obtaining.

After that, she contacted the museum and offered her services gratis, just to gain experience. The museum had some human archaeological reproductions that they permitted her to practice on. The results were startling, so much so that Nathan offered her a part-time job in the art department and promised her a full-time position after graduation. She accepted Nathan's offer and began work immediately after graduation as an assistant display designer until the first forensic project came along. She began to do reconstructions for real when the Town Creek Indian project was approved a year and a half later and the museum was contacted by the University of North Carolina anthropology department to work in concert with their research. The entire ceremonial mound had been excavated as an ongoing project begun back in 1937 and continued as a research site and restored village now open to the public at the Town Creek museum. Several Native American skeletons unearthed from the burial pits had been selected for the first facial reconstructions and Devon gained instant recognition for her unusual and seldom heard of skill as a reconstruction artist. It was very exciting, and Devon was proud to be part of such an important project.

After the Town Creek project, the opportunities for Devon to practice her skills as a forensic sculptor were sporadic, but her reputation as one of only a few artists in the country able to do this pro-

cedure secured a certain security for her job at the museum. It
was through a feature article in the newspaper about women with
unusual careers that Detective Whyte got the idea to contact Devon
for his case and called her a few weeks later. The article spotlighted
Devon's forensic reconstructions for the museum and Detective Whyte
was inspired by the life-like detail he saw in the photos of her work.

As Devon began the tedious task of precisely measuring and cutting the tissue thickness markers, she began to wonder for the first
time who this person was. It must be awful for his family to have
spent every holiday wondering what happened to him. And it was
cruel of him not to leave a note telling why, and at the very least to
apologize for the pain he had caused them. What kind of dire circumstances would cause a man of obvious means to throw himself
to his death? What were his thoughts as he fell? Relief? Regret? She
turned the music up louder. "Just work, don't think," she scolded.

She cut thirty or so tissue depth markers, varying in thickness
from 4 mm to 20 mm. Pencil eraser refills worked perfectly as soft
little dowels that could easily be sliced with a razor blade and carefully glued to even the narrowest facial bones. Precision was key to
the success of the sculpt. The scar on her index finger reminded her
that a wandering mind and razor blades were less than a winning
combination. She started measuring with the surgical caliper and
marking the tubular eraser with fine lines where she would slice the
thinnest markers. Markers #4, 1, 11, and 2, would be glued to the
forehead and nasal bridge.

Each marker corresponded to a strategic position on the face.
There were several charts that showed variations in tissue thick-

TISSUE THICKNESS CHART (MALE)

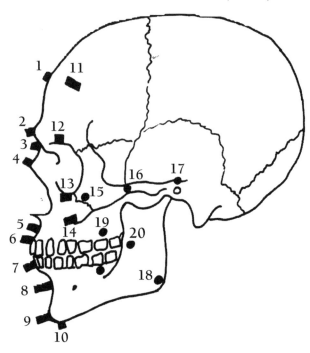

No.	Midline Measurement (millimeters)	
1	Hairline	4.25
2	Glabella	5.25
3	Nasion	6.50
4	Nasal Bridge	3.00
5	Mid Philtrum	10.00
6	Upper Lip Margin	9.75
7	Lower Lip Margin	11.00
8	Chin-Lip Fold	10.75
9	Chin Eminence	11.25
10	Under Chin	7.25

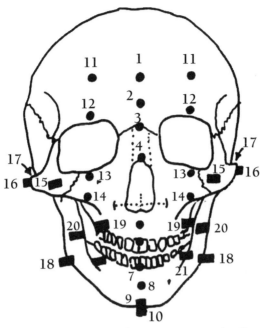

No.	Bilateral Measurement (millimeters)	
11	Frontal Eminence	4.25
12	Supraorbital	8.25
13	Suborbital	5.75
14	Inferior Malar	13.50
15	Lateral Orbit	9.75
16	Zygomatic Arch	7.00
17	Supraglenoid	8.25
18	Gonial angle	11.00
19	Supra M2	18.50
20	Occlusal Line	17.75
21	Sub M2	15.25

* From Kollmann and Buchly, 1898
* References: Gerasimov, M.M. THE FACE FINDER (J.B. Lippincott, Philadelphia and New York, 1971)

ness for the average male and female, as well as average tissue thickness for other races. She placed the tissue chart labeled _(AVERAGE/ CAUCASIAN MALE)_ in front of her for easy reference. The earliest attempts at determining average tissue depth on the face were rather crude. In 1898, two researchers named Kollmann and Buchly, inserted a needle blackened with soot from a candle, into the facial tissue of cadavers, and measured the area where the soot had been wiped clean when the needle was removed. Ultra sound was the most popular method of measuring tissue thickness in recent years, and Devon had heard about even more sophisticated methods used today such as 3D computer imaging.

She focused on her work, meticulously cutting the erasers until she finished up with markers #19, 20, and 21. These were the thickest and easiest markers to cut and would be placed along the back section of the jaw line.

It was 9:00 P.M., and Devon was at a good stopping point. She was ready to get home and relax. Although she had made a good start to her work that evening by cutting the markers, she still had not touched the skull. Everything she had done so far was merely preparation. She had to admit to herself that she had taken procrastination to new heights. It was only a matter of time before she would have to reach into the box, cradle her hands around the skull to lift it out, and hope that she would be spared any psychic epiphany regarding this man.

She stretched her arms, rubbed the nape of her neck, and arched her back in a catlike motion. She straightened up her work area one more time and returned Dana's walkman to her desk drawer. On her way out, an unexpected burst of energy compelled her to take the Broad Street exit stairs two at a time. "Twenty-six, twenty-eight, thirty, thirty-two." She caught herself doing it again.

Outside, the night air was cool and the streets were quiet. Devon closed her eyes and took in a deep, satisfying breath. The buses ran every fifteen minutes, and if she was lucky she could catch the 9:15 and be home and tucked in bed by 10:30. An elderly lady standing next to her at the bus stop wearily clutched a tote bag filled with various cleaning supplies. They exchanged smiles and Devon was struck with a sudden sense of gratitude for her job, reminding herself that, although she took home a meager salary, she really had nothing to complain about.

～

The next day Devon decided to pack a second lunch so she could just stay late after work and not go back and forth. The fewer buses the better. She also packed several of her own cassette tapes. Dana's taste in music was not exactly mainstream. Flash-in-the-pan groups like *The Gagging Maggots* and *Nervosa* were just too "out there" for Devon. She'd take classic rock n' roll any day of the week.

At five o'clock, Dana, Michelle, and a few other artists stopped by as they were leaving to wish her luck with the reconstruction. She took a short break, had a chocolate bar, and then went over to her work table. Dana had left her walkman out in plain view with a note stuck to it that read, "You forgot to say please, but go ahead and use it anyway. D."

"Smart aleck," Devon grumbled. She was going to ask permission, she just hadn't gotten around to it yet.

There it was. Waiting for her. The brown box. In exactly the same place she had left it the night before. She shuffled her sculpting tools around, opened up several boxes of clay, straightened the row of markers for the third time, and realized she couldn't think of anything else she could do to avoid the box. She reached over and took a deep breath and opened it.

"Okay, there's nothing new in there—just old bones," she reassured herself. Her palms were moist and her face felt hot, but she was ready. She reached both hands into the box, closed her eyes, and gently cupped the skull from underneath and lifted it up. The surface was smooth and it weighed, she guessed, about two pounds. With her eyes still closed tight she stood motionless and waited. *Dizzy?* No. *Tingly?* No. *Anything?* No. By now something would have happened. Nothing! Nothing was happening. It was just an ordinary skull made of ordinary bones and teeth. She felt triumphant.

"Breathe, Devon. Time to breathe," she laughed. "Oh God, thank you," she said with heartfelt relief. With her spirits lifted and her fears circumvented, she was downright enthusiastic about completing this project. How could she have been so ridiculous, making such a big deal out of taking this case? She was proud of herself now. And Milly would be too.

The skull fit nicely on the metal armature, and she secured it from wobbling with the attached fasteners. With the skull in place, Devon was ready to begin the second step of gluing the markers onto the skull. She used an acetone soluble cement which facilitated easy removal of the markers without damage to the skull when the sculpt was dismantled. Starting with the first marker, she dabbed a small amount of glue on the bottom of it and pressed it in place. This step was, without question, the easiest. Every reconstruction she did started out the same but ended otherwise. She always felt a little anxiety that the face she was currently working on might resemble the previous bust. It was a warning held over from art school that all sculptors subconsciously incorporated aspects of their own facial features into their work. When she looked back at each reconstruction she had completed over the years, it wasn't too hard to see telltale signs of her own upper eyelid or the curl at the corners of her lips subtly sculpted into the clay.

"I can't get no. . . uh, uh, uh. . . no SA—TIS—FAK—SHUN, oh no, no, no . . ." she sang as she waited for the glue to dry under the markers. This was going great. She was feeling so positive she decided to give Dr. Florio a call and invite him to have a "look-see." And if he didn't have to rush home to his wife's pot roast, maybe she would invite him to stay and watch her work.

When all the markers had been glued in position, she began to cut narrow strips of clay about three-quarters of an inch wide that would be attached to the skull in between the markers, connecting the dots.

She fantasized as she cut the flesh-colored, *Plasticine* modeling clay, that Detective Whyte would congratulate her on the superb job she had done. He would be so impressed. And the victim's family would shower her with gratitude for finding their long-lost loved one. There would be newspaper articles with pictures, TV, interviews, and, of course, Nathan would be the first to tell her the good news of her promotion and raise! The future was looking bright.

It was still early when she dialed Dr. Florio's number. She had her lines all prepared but when she heard his voice on the other end it was only a recording. He had already gone home. She waited for the beep and then began.

"James, this is Devon. Good news! I'm making excellent progress on the reconstruction. I've changed my mind and would like to invite you to come by the museum tomorrow evening while I'm working. Give me a call at my office if you like or just be at the back entrance at 7:00 P.M. and I'll let you in. See you soon." Click.

She continued cutting strips of clay. The warmth of her fingers softened the modeling clay and made it easy to wedge the strips between the markers. She would match the thickness of clay to the depth of the markers, creating a latticework that would cover the entire skull, and form a vented mask.

Devon followed the facial diagrams and skillfully curved the pieces of clay around the contours of the cranium, along the supraglenoid and zygomatic arch, and across the lateral orbits, and stopping at the inferior malar. Strip after strip was set in place until almost half the face was connected. Later on, when all of the blank spaces were eventually filled in with clay, the foundation of the face would be laid. It was going great. She had never accomplished so much in so little time. As the clay filled in the spaces, the first glimpses of his face began to appear. She made a few entries in her journal regarding her swift progress and her first impressions of what this man might look like.

Tuesday, October 3

Reconstruction is going great. No problems—none! Markers cut, glued, and vented mask begun. Partial mask indicates high cheekbones, strong chin, somewhat angular face. Nasal aperture and nasal spine measurements indicate prominent nose. Good genes— we should all be so lucky!

*note: contact Steve for appointment to shoot progress photos for files.

She draped a clean sheet of opaque plastic over the bust, packed up her things, and said "good-night" to her anonymous acquaintance.

～

*A*ll day Wednesday, Devon waited to hear from James Florio. She was in and out of planning meetings for a Civil War exhibit that was to open in the spring. She checked her voice mail periodically. No messages. He must be having a really busy day.

By 4:30 her disappointment was written all over her face. Nathan asked her if she was staying late again to work on the project. "Yes, it's going well and I hope to deliver it to Detective Whyte in ten days."

In the studio, a few hours later, Devon studied the expressionless visage before her, and noticed that one ear was slightly higher than the other. Minor adjustment. She peeled off the left ear, lowered it no more than an eighth of an inch, and reattached it to the bust. Now it looked right. She filled in the remaining areas with clay until the entire surface of the facial bones was covered except for the anterior nasal and orbital apertures. One cotton ball was placed in each eye socket and one in the nasal aperture. The bones in the nasal cavity were very fragile and some as thin as paper. The cotton balls protected these delicate areas from being clogged with clay that might break off parts of the bone when removed. The eye sockets were less fragile, but the cotton acted as a protective barrier for the same reason. With these steps completed, she decided to begin work on the nose.

Devon measured the nasal aperture at its widest point near the bottom of the opening. She could determine the width of his nose by adding 10mm to the first measurement (5 mm to each side). The nostrils follow the line of the aperture. This was the standard calculation for Caucasians. It varied slightly with other races. In order to determine the projection of his nose, she measured a small ridge called the nasal spine that ran from the front of the nasal opening straight back toward the skull cavity. It was rare that this fragile bone was ever completely intact, but usually enough of it was there to make a decent measurement and a respectable guess as to its original size. The projection of the nose equaled three times the length of the nasal spine. In this case, the nasal spine was in good condition and she measured 4mm along the ridge. She cut a strip of clay 6–8mm wide and four times the length of the spine; approximately 24 mm in length. She then placed one fourth the length of the clay strip over the nasal spine with the rest of the remaining strip projecting outward. Small beads of clay no larger than capers were then used to fill in the rest of the nasal aperture and as this was completed the shape of the nose became apparent. Devon picked up a sculpting tool and used it to press the beads of clay into the spaces that were too small for her fingers to work. The basic shape was there, but she would not do the final smoothing and add her finishing touches until all the soft tissue parts, ears, nose, eyes, lips, were roughed out. She then measured the length of the nose and compared it to the length of one ear. Generally, the length of the nose equaled the length of the ear. Just another minor adjustment which took her a few minutes to correct.

She looked at her watch and decided it was still early enough to at least start on the mouth. It took a great deal of time to sculpt the lips so they looked soft and natural. Only the eyes required an even greater attention to detail. She wondered what kind of lips Dr. Florio had.

Typically, the width of the mouth matched the span of the front six teeth. With her calipers she measured the distance between two lines radiating out from the junction of the canine and first premolar on each side. The clay was pliable and easy to manipulate as Devon patted and pushed and scraped it around the mouth, leaving the teeth exposed. She would add the lips much later. What would this man tell her about his death if he could? Was he jilted by a lover? It was safe to ponder his demise now that there seemed to be no connection to her.

At 6:50 she took a break and paged through a magazine. She was disappointed in the way the day was turning out. She really had thought that Dr. Florio would return her call, but now it was obvious he was not going to. Her only consolation was the thought that he was probably married, anyway. At 7:00 P.M. Devon went to the rest room and decided to check the back door on the off chance that James had showed up. When she opened the door, to her surprise, he was standing there.

"Am I late?" he asked.

"Oh geez, no. I . . . I'm just suprised to see you." She was embarrassed. "I didn't hear from you today, so I guess I thought you were too busy, but I'm glad you came." She was babbling, she berated herself. "I'm Devon," she said finally.

"James. Nice to meet you," he answered. "I'm eager to see what you've done so far."

"Well, come on, I'll show you," she said. He followed her up the stairs, and she wondered if her derriere looked like a doublewide in her khakis.

Devon was delighted to have the company—especially Dr. Florio's. He was not at all what she pictured but exactly what she liked. Rugged and outdoorsy, handsome in an earthy way. Most physicians she knew took on a sickly pallor from working endless hours under fluorescent hospital lights. But James was tanned and looked as though he had just returned from a backcountry expedition.

As he reached to open the stairwell door for her, she glanced at his hands. Specifically, his left hand. No ring. Good sign. They walked through the museum chatting casually about their jobs until they reached the artists' studio. He walked over to the work-in-progress and politely waited for her to join him.

The reconstruction, with its hollow eye sockets and bared teeth, would have looked hideous to someone unfamiliar with forensic medicine. It was even a little scary to Devon if she stared at it too long. But James performed autopsies every day in cases that ranged from "suspicious" natural causes to blatant homicide. He had seen it all—the real thing, not just clay faces. And he had probably handled more bones and body parts than she could imagine.

The doctor asked her questions about the process and her initial pursuit learning to do it. She gladly told him the whole story. He was so likable and easy to talk to—they really clicked. Devon thought they could definitely be friends—and perhaps more.

"I was going to order in a pepperoni with extra cheese. Would you like to stick around and have a slice or two?" she asked. Before he could answer she interjected, "How silly of me, you probably need to get home to help the kids with their homework." She regretted the obviousness of the comment the minute it slipped from her mouth.

"Well, yes, and after that I have to chop some wood so I can make a fire to keep my ailing grandmother warm," he teased. "I'm divorced, I don't have any children, and I'd love a pizza—with black olives." He smiled.

The evening flew by and Devon had gotten very little work done on the reconstruction since Dr. Florio's arrival. They ate pizza and talked until 10:00 P.M. When he found out she was without a car, he insisted on giving her a ride home. As he pulled up to her building, she realized she hated for the evening to end. It had been so long since Devon had met a man with whom she had so much in common. James was intelligent, fun to be around, and genuinely interested in her work. Had she known this project was going to be so full of opportunities, she would have said yes immediately, and sent a bouquet of "thank you" flowers to Detective Whyte.

"Thanks for the ride home, James."

"No problem. I really enjoyed this evening. Sorry I slowed you down, though," he apologized.

"Actually, you did me a favor. I needed a break. Would you like to see it again after he has a little more of his face?" she laughed.

"You bet. Give me a call at the hospital and we'll work it out. Good night."

Devon watched as he drove away and knew there was no way she was going to get to sleep tonight. She was premature in thinking that this brief evening with Dr. Florio predicted a romantic future. She didn't care. She was too happy to worry about reality. She bounded up the stairs two at a time and prayed that Milly would still be up.

"Eighteen, twenty, twenty-two, . . . not even out of breath," she bragged to herself.

There was a sliver of amber light coming from under Milly's door. "Great, she's up." Devon pressed her ear to the door and heard "La Boheme" playing softly in the background. She rapped lightly and waited.

"Everything okay?" Milly asked, slightly alarmed, as she cracked open the door.

"Okay?? No, everything is not okay," she said, straight-faced. "Everything is fantastic! Milly, you wouldn't believe what kind of day I've had." Her face was beaming now, and she was dying to tell her friend about Dr. Florio.

"Well, should I put on the tea or break out a bottle of wine?" Milly asked as she ushered Devon into the living room.

"Wine, definitely wine."

They curled up in their favorite respective chairs and Milly poured two large glasses of white wine. Devon was so grateful to have a friend with whom she could share these moments.

"Okay Devon, I'm all ears, " Milly grinned.

Devon started from the top, telling how she had begun "hands-on" work with the skull and was so far free of any visions or intuitions. That she was excited about the project now and anticipated an early completion. When she got to the part about Dr. Florio, she was grinning from ear to ear. Not one detail of his physical appearance was left out. Milly was happy for her and told her that she hoped something would come of it. Devon teased that maybe he had an older brother for Milly, and at that, Milly sprayed out her chardonnay in a burst of laughter. They talked on and on until Milly's yawns were less than two minutes apart. The second bottle of wine just seemed to evaporate. They each had one last night-cap. Alka Seltzer. Devon hugged her friend tight, thanked her for staying up so late to listen, and stumbled back to her apartment.

She plopped into bed, not even brushing her teeth or washing her face, and thereby breaking the cardinal rules of good hygiene. Her mother would faint. Devon smiled at the thought and decided she rather enjoyed being a rebel.

$\sim$

*E*very pothole the bus bounced over felt like a two-mile caldera to her pounding headache. She had forgot what a hangover felt like. In fact, she wasn't really sure she had ever had one. *I hope Milly's doing better than I am.* But Milly didn't have to go to work like Devon did. She could sleep late if she wanted, then later make a hot cup of tea and slowly try to coax her tongue and her brain into working simultaneously. It had come to seem natural that Milly stayed in her apartment most of the time, caring for her plants, reading, and listening to music. She lived simply and never seemed to want for anything, and she never, ever talked about money. Every now and then Devon's curiosity tempted her to ask Milly where her income came from, but then she would hear her mother remind her that discretion was the better part of valor, and she would not ask. A while ago, in one of their earliest conversations, Milly referred to one of her "students," so Devon assumed that she was a retired teacher. It must have been challenging to collect all those wonderful antiques on a teacher's salary.

"Tenth and Broad Street," the bus driver called out. Devon hung onto the backs of the seats and pulled her way up the aisle. Why was everyone talking so loudly this morning? Her stomach was queasy and her tongue felt like her bathroom carpet. She stopped at the bus driver's seat and glanced over at him. He was smiling. "Have a nice day, now."

On any other day she would have taken his pleasant comment as just that, but today she questioned whether or not he was being sarcastic. He could probably see that she had too much to drink the night before and seemed to enjoy watching her wince at every bump and curve. She peered out over her sunglasses and started to say something smart, but instead replied with a simple "Thanks."

Thursday was a nightmarish day. Her workload was heavy and she barely had time for lunch. The headache was almost gone by 2:00 that afternoon, but her energy tank was almost on empty.

"Hey Devon, Lori and I are headed out to the bargain movie theater tonight after work. Why don't you join us? We're going to grab a couple of burgers afterwards. It'll be fun," Beth suggested enthusiastically.

Beth and Lori were twins who worked in acquisitions. They were an amazing team. Upbeat, energetic, smart, and totally organized. It was like having one brain in two bodies, working harmoniously and going in two different directions when needed. They did everything together and often included her in their "girls' night out" plans. Devon admired their sunny personalities, but sometimes their simultaneous answers and identical rapid-fire giggling drove her up the wall. "Gee, Beth, I'll have to pass for tonight." She continued, "I'm working late on a special project, but thanks anyway." However, even if she wasn't working on her "*special project,*" tonight would have been out of the question. She was exhausted from the night before and all she could think about was sleep. Beth shrugged her shoulders in that perky way of hers and said maybe next time.

It looked like there was about one cup of coffee left in the bottom of the pot and Devon went for it. She wished she had gotten more work done on the reconstruction last evening, then she wouldn't have to stay so late tonight. But Detective Whyte had called her once already that week to see how things were going, and she felt pressured. If she wanted to complete the sculpt on her proposed schedule, she had to work tonight.

The coffee was a little burned and tasted bitter. It was hot, though, and Devon knew the caffeine would kick in any moment. She busied herself for the next couple of hours catching up on paperwork that Nathan was waiting for. Before she knew it, everyone was clearing their desks to go home. Some saint had made another pot of coffee. She carried her coffee mug as though it were a chalice as she walked wearily over to the java altar and filled it to the top, silently giving thanks.

Time to make a face.

The measurements for the eye sockets ran diagonally across one corner of the orbit to the other. Then two more measurements top to bottom, and side to side that intersected in the middle. This intersection determined where the pupil would be centered. She formed two balls of clay, approximately twenty-four millimeters each in diameter, and attached the prosthetic eye caps to them. It was tricky to place the eyeballs in the sockets and get them lined up evenly, because if she didn't the poor guy might end up looking like a flounder. One trick she had learned was to align the pupils with the corners of the mouth and the widest points of the chin. She tested all this out when she was first learning by measuring her own features. It worked.

Even though this was a tedious and time consuming step, it was still fairly simple. The difficult part was constructing and shaping the eyelids to appear as lifelike as possible. If the eyes were not done just right, the facial expression would appear frightened, or angry, or sleepy. It took hours of infinitesimal adjustments and manipulations of the clay to find that perfect balance in which the eyelids hung over the iris but above the pupil and presented a peaceful, relaxed expression. This was Devon's special talent. All of her reconstructions appeared so lifelike they looked as though they might speak at any given moment. The marriage of intuition and artistic talent took on a life force of its own and guided her hands to shape the clay into remarkably realistic faces. Devon wondered if she had the energy to wrestle with this step of the procedure tonight, but she decided she had no choice.

She ate a snack from the vending machine and felt a little better, but twenty minutes later she was even more tired than before.

"Maybe I'll just put my head down for a few minutes before I start the eyelids," she said as she rested her head on her arm. "Just a few minutes . . ." and she closed her eyes.

~

The dream was odd. Devon was climbing stairs. Endless stairs. It was dark and she was frightened, but something compelled her to go on. There were flashes of bright light but she was unable to see anything around her. More steps. Bright light. The air was damp, and when she placed her hand on the wall to steady herself, it felt cold. She kept climbing and then she saw a shadowy outline of someone in front of her. No one answered when she called out. She became frightened and then suddenly she could see someone falling through the darkness. She had no idea where she was. The light flashed again and a man's voice shouted harshly at her, "Hey—hey you, what are you doing in here?" It was so real. Then again, "Hey, you're not supposed to be in here," and then, "C'mon, wake up," and she felt someone shaking her shoulder.

Devon jerked up out of her sleep and saw a security guard hovering over her with a scowl on his face and his flashlight in his hand. He was obviously perturbed and asked her again, "I said, . . . what are you doing in here at 8:30 at night? Nobody told me anything about people being in here after hours."

Devon was rattled. What an awful dream. How long had she been asleep? It seemed like a few minutes but the wall clock told her it had been more like an hour. She quickly wiped the little puddle of drool off her arm and stared up at the guard.

The night guards usually worked special events and weekends only. "Who are you?" she asked. "Where's Burnie? What are you doing here tonight?" Mr. Burns was a silver-haired retiree whom everyone affectionately called "Burnie." He was soft spoken and shy and worked part-time as a security guard to supplement his social security income. Burnie was fond of Devon because she always treated him with respect and kindness. When he was working at special functions, she would make up a plate of food for him from the buffet table so he could eat when he was on break. Occasionally, she would sneak him a glass of champagne or wine, even though they both risked losing their jobs had he been caught. Devon didn't think one little glass would hurt. And of course, Burnie agreed.

"I don't know any Burnie. I'm Franklin Greene, night watchman. Started today. Now look here—do you have permission to be in here? Nobody said nothin' to me about people creeping around here at night."

Creeping around? If anybody was creeping around it was him, she thought sourly.

"Yes, of course, I have permission to be here. Don't you see I'm working on something?" she asked and then realized how ridiculous that sounded since he had just awakened her from a sound sleep. She changed the subject. "Since when are night guards on duty during the week?"

"Since now. Look missy, I don't keep up with company policy changes. I just report to work. I'll need to get your name," he said as he pulled out a little note pad.

"My name is Devon Gardiner," she said flatly.

"How long you supposed to be here tonight?" he asked.

Devon wanted to give him a piece of her mind for being so rude to her but once again her insecurity held her back. "Oh, probably just another hour or so. Maybe 9:00 to 9:30 at the latest."

"Hmm . . . okay, then. I guess that'd be all right." As he turned to leave, his flashlight beam danced over her face, blinding her for a second. He continued to walk out the door, flashing the light back and forth as though he were looking for the enemy in the jungles of Vietnam.

"What a mutant!" she said aloud after he closed the door and was well out of hearing range. She wondered how many, if any, of his ancestors were even bipedal.

In a way, though, Devon was glad for the intrusion. She was wide awake now and could still get quite a bit of the eyes done before she went home. Tomorrow she was going to ask Nathan why Burnie wasn't assigned. She must have missed the announcement regarding the new policy at the staff meeting. No wonder — she was so out of it this morning there was no telling what else she missed.

She cut four strips of clay about a half-inch wide, two inches long, and only one-sixteenth of an inch thick, and laid them on the table. Two upper eyelids and two lower. These were gently pressed into the crease between the upper eyelid and the fleshy area under the eyebrow and then below each eye from the inside near the bridge of the nose to the outer end toward the temple. It was easier to keep the thickness uniform by using a rosewood sculpting tool to press the clay into position rather than to use her fingers. Even the slightest bit of excess pressure would thin out the clay and make the lids appear uneven and she would have to do it again. It was so delicate, it usually took a few tries, anyway. After that she proceeded to deftly adjust the curvature of the lids, making sure they hung evenly over the eye caps. With both hands resting on the face, she leaned back into her chair to scrutinize her work so far.

Although his face was barely put together and none of the features smoothed out, Devon could tell this man would stick out in a crowd. She was confident that when she was finished, anyone still out there who knew him, would be able to recognize him from the sculpt.

Then it began. She shuddered convulsively and began to tremble. The tingling in her fingers ran all the way up her arms, and her eyes rolled back. When she tried to remove her hands from the skull she could not. Her whole body was frozen in place but her mind was racing forward into the unknown. She was terrified. A moment later she could see again but nothing looked familiar. She had entered someone else's world. His world. And like it or not, she was about to be witness to the events that surrounded his death.

IV

~

MACK

~

1950

"Now hold on, Mr. Winborne," Mack stammered. "You got the wrong idea 'bout what's goin' on here."

"Don't move," Winborne commanded in a steady voice. "I can see exactly what's going on."

Mack came out from behind the desk and started to move toward his angry employer. "No sir, I don't think you do."

"If you take one more step, I'll blow your head off."

Mack ignored his warning and moved a little closer, talking all the while. His hands were in the air and he spoke a little quieter this time. "Mr. Winborne, please, just listen to me for one minute. I come up here to the house to talk to you about keepin' my job, that's all. The door was open so I just come in. I saw you upstairs and called out to you, but you didn't answer me." He took two more steps as slowly as he could, keeping eye contact with Winborne the whole time. "And then I come upstairs to wait for you, ya' see? Then, I seen your briefcase—and well, I just wanted to see what was in it." He was only a few feet in front of the shotgun now, and he stopped. "You can count the money. I didn't take nothin'—not a red cent, honest."

"Honest? Did you say honest? I catch you red-handed in my office, with your hands on my money, and you say you're honest? You must really think me the fool! I assure you, young man, I am not."

Mack could see the rage in his eyes, and how his temples were pulsing. This man was going to pull the trigger and kill him, and no one would ever question what had happened. It would be an open-and-shut case of a lowlife drifter who broke into a high-society mansion and tried to steal money. Winborne would claim self-defense—case closed. His finger was tightening on the trigger, and Mack's survival instincts took over.

He lunged forward with the same agility and speed as a few weeks earlier when he saved the old man from his fall, only this time he was leaping to save his own skin. He tackled Winborne at his midsection, well below the gun barrel. The force of his weight and the suddenness of his actions caught Winborne off guard, and the gun flew out of his hands and landed on the floor. It did not go off. However, as the two men collided, they fell backward through the doorway and across the narrow hall. Mack's left foot caught in the balcony railing, and he jerked to a stop. Unfortunately, Winborne continued moving and went tumbling headfirst toward the top step. His eyes bulged wide with fear and for a split second met with the younger man's frozen gaze. Mack saw the look of a man who knew death was about to embrace him. Even if he had thought of it, he could not have gotten back up on his own feet in time to reach out, grab Winborne, and save him. Instead, Mack watched as his body tumbled and flopped down the winding marble staircase like a rag doll, finally to lie motionless at the bottom. He wished the old man had listened to him, at least given him a chance. Mack got up, went back into the office, and looked around. It appeared very little had been moved out of place in the scuffle, but he took his time to make sure. He prided himself on his ability to keep his wits in a crisis and cover his tracks. It had always been Bobby's reckless temper and penchant for smashing things that had gotten them into trouble in the past.

The Winchester model 12 was still on the floor. If anyone found the gun loaded, it would be a red flag for sure. He picked it up, released the slide lock, and waited for the bolt to fall back. But there was nothing to unload. The chamber and magazine were empty. The old man pulled a pretty good bluff but lost the gamble. It was a down-right shame. Mack knew all too well how suddenly one's luck could change. But there was no time for sentiment, now.

He propped the gun behind the door, grabbed the briefcase, and ran back down the stairs to see if Winborne were alive. When he checked the man's pulse it was pitifully weak, at best. Winborne was unconscious, barely breathing. Then his eyes opened and he managed a strangled gasp and died.

6:57 A.M. He had just enough time to get out of there. Mack peered out the front doors. All clear. He removed Winborne's tweed jacket and slipped it on. Then he picked up the body and the briefcase and moved quickly toward the car. His movements were jerky, and he kept looking behind him, taking a moment to listen for the sounds of the house servants as they filed into the mansion to report for work. They would enter through the back door, and he was counting on that extra minute or two. All quiet. The car was still running. No one in sight.

Mack managed to open the back door of the car and to lay the body and the briefcase on the floor between the front and back seats. He hopped into the driver's seat and started slowly down the gravel driveway toward the main gate. There was a gray wool cap lying on the front seat next to him. He put it on and pulled it down low on his forehead. Mack prayed that all the employees had not yet left breakfast for their posts. If they had, any one of them might walk out from behind the hedgerows and recognize him. It was a long drive from the manor house to the main gate. Would his luck hold? His life depended on it.

Mack could see the main gate in the distance. It looked clear. "Drive steady — don't speed," he told himself. He approached the automatic gate and slowed down to allow it to open fully. His hands were slippery with sweat, and he kept checking the rear mirror. Would he make it? His heart was pounding. He was so close. A mixture of excitement, fear, disbelief, and regret swirled around inside him. He had certainly not planned for things to go this badly. But now he was forced to make the best of a bad situation, as he had had to do so many times before. As he went through the gate, he saw in the rearview mirror one of the groundsmen standing in the drive-way, watching him drive away. He didn't dare stop but rolled down the window and gave a casual wave as though he were going out for the Sunday paper. The small man stood there a moment longer, scratched his head, and finally turned back to his work.

Josè could not figure it out. In all the years he had worked there, he had never seen Mr. Winborne wave good-bye from the car to any-one—not even Danielle.

~

*F*or the next hour and a half, Mack drove with no partic-ular destination in mind. Eventually, he calmed down and realized he had to dump the body and make a plan. There was a sign along the road that read "*To Linville Caverns.*" That sounded like an ideal place to hide a body. He remembered hearing Audra Gallagher, the butler's daughter, tell a scary story about the bottomless pits and un-explored caverns that ran deep through a section of the Blue Ridge mountains called Linville Caverns. She was the care-taker for some of the house staff's children and had them sitting on the lawn in front of her. Mack was on his way back to the maintenance shed when he caught the sounds of children gasping in exaggerated fear and then giggling with the anticipation of more. He couldn't help but get caught up in Audra's charismatic storytelling. And now her little story was going to save his skin.

When he arrived, however, park guides and tourists with noisy kids were milling around the entrance. How would he ever sneak a well-dressed corpse past all these people? It was impossible during the day. If he came back after closing, when it was dark, he might be able to sneak in, go down one of the "off-limits" corridors to an unexplored cave, and drop the body into a bottomless pit. Now he was thinking. He turned the car around and left. A couple of miles down the road, he took a right onto a dirt lane. This was the worst situation Mack had ever gotten himself into and he prayed he could get himself out of it. After about twenty minutes more, he stopped. The road seemed safe enough; he hadn't seen a single car on it except his. He was tired and hungry. He decided to sleep for a few hours and then get something to eat while he waited for the sun to go down.

The sound of a dog barking frantically awakened him with a start. Up on his hind legs, slobbering all over Mack's window, was a large coon hound announcing to anyone within earshot that something was awry. Mack looked out the front window of the car to see in the distance the dog's owner walking down the middle of the dusty road toward him. He swung around and looked over the seat at the body, still crumpled there and totally exposed. He had to head this guy off before he ever reached the car.

"Go on—git down and shut up," he said to the dog as he tried to open the car door. But the weight of the dog's body pushed the door closed again as Mack watched the man getting closer and closer to the car. "God dammit, I said git off," he hissed the second time, shoving the door open so hard the dog flew backward and landed on his back, then scurried yelping back to his owner.

"Hey," Mack called out to the wrinkled old man in as friendly a tone as he could muster. "Hey" was universal southern speak for "hello" and he hoped this would identify him as a local—or at least friendly. No answer. Mack had heard many stories that mountain folk were not known for welcoming strangers who trespassed on their land, and he was uneasy. He kept walking until they were about ten feet apart and a good twenty feet from the car. The man in the denim overalls and stained tee shirt looked hard at Mack as he stroked his fingers up and down the barrel of his shotgun. Mack tried again. "Hey, I reckon I took a wrong turn here somewhere. I'd be mighty grateful if you could point me the way to Linville Gorge," he said politely. Mack wasn't sure if the man was buying it, but the dog was definitely suspicious. He had begun howling and barking again. The greasy-haired man spat out a stream of tobacco-stained saliva, looked him in the eye, then at the car, and back again at Mack. When he finally opened his mouth to speak, he displayed a mass of yellowish, rotten teeth that were piled on top of each other like a litter of newborn pups. "What'd you say you was lookin' for?" he asked in a slow voice.

"Linville Gorge. I hear it's a right pretty sight."

"Uh-huh . . . where'd you say you was from?" The dog was still whining and was really starting to annoy Mack.

"Spruce Pine. Yes sir, born and raised there," Mack lied. "Now if you could just give me them directions, I'll be on my way."

"Uh-huh." The man started to laugh and scratched his chin. He surprised Mack with his perceptiveness. "Look sonny, I don't know what you's up to and I don't right much care. But I know'd plenty a folks from Spruce Pine and they don't talk nothin like you. If I was a bettin' man—I'd guess you's from down east." He had Mack's full attention and continued. "I don't like trouble, so I'm gonna be right neighborly and point you on yer way. Understand?" Mack nodded and the old man continued. "Go on back down this here road and take yer third left. You'll see it. Now you best git goin. Some people round here ain't as friendly as me," he said with a crafty smile.

"Thank you, now." Mack said as he hurried back to the car. The dog took one last nip at his ankle but missed, and the old man cackled. In spite of the old-timer's appearance, he turned out to be helpful and anything but a backwoods dolt. Nevertheless, it didn't matter whether someone was friendly or not, Mack knew if they saw Winborne's body, his number would be up. Before he did anything else he had to dump the body. His stomach ached with hunger but that would have to wait until he had things under control again.

Despite his nerve-wracking encounter with the mountaineer, the sleep had rejuvenated him. *Did he say the second or the third left?* Mack didn't remember passing any little roads on his way in. He must have been too nervous to notice. "I think it was the second left," he said to himself and turned down the road. It didn't look familiar at all, and after a few more miles, Mack knew he was on the wrong road. "Damn, must have been the third left."

The road had narrowed so much at this point that there was nowhere to turn the car around. A small, hand-painted, sign read "*Dead End.*" Maybe he could turn around up ahead. A minute later Mack pulled the car to the very edge of the mountain road, careful not to back into the ditch, and managed to turn the car around. He stopped the car and walked over to the bushes to relieve himself.

A small animal rustled in the mountain laurel scrub, and he tried to see what it was. Instead, he saw an overgrown footpath that led into the woods. It dawned on him that maybe he didn't need to go all the way back to Linville Caverns to dump Winborne's body.

He followed the path into the woods a way, and it was obvious that no one had set foot on it for quite some time. It came to an abrupt end at a steep rock wall on the side of the mountain. In front of him was another sign that read "*J.R. Surles Gem Mine—CLOSED —No Trespassin.*" He had heard the servants at the mansion talk about the gem mines in that area—mostly just small rubies and sapphires—but he had never really believed it until now. Once or twice he had thought about panning for gems but never got around to it. Besides, gemstones were too hard to unload. He had something much more valuable—a briefcase full of cold hard cash.

The entrance to the mine had caved in and was clogged with large boulders and debris. The remaining entry space was boarded over with old barn wood. Over the years, some of the wood had rotted and the rest had shrunk so that the rusted nails protruded from the surface. It had possibilities if he could make his way in. Mack began tearing at the boards. Some came off easier than others, but he was determined to get inside. It took less than fifteen minutes for him to open up a hole and crawl into the mine shaft. The air was dank and heavy and it smelled stale. He flicked his lighter to get a better look. It would be a tight fit, but he thought he could cram Winborne through the opening and drag him as far into the cave as possible, bury him with a few rocks, and get out of town. It was foolproof. He was almost home free. To bad he didn't have this kind of luck at the race track.

Mack hurried back to the car to get the body. He didn't remember Winborne being so heavy. Maybe it was the guilt that weighed so much. Ridiculous. He put the corpse on the ground and decided to drag it by the feet rather than carry it down the footpath. That allowed him to walk facing forward where he could avoid seeing the old man's ashen face and touching the cold flesh. He could not, however, avoid hearing the dull thumping sound as Winborne's head occasionally bumped over a rock or fallen tree limb.

The money was the only thing that kept Mack from falling apart.

He had become a thief through no choice of his own, but he was not a murderer. He kept telling himself it would all be over in a few short hours, and he intended never to look back.

Once inside the mine, he crawled as far as he could on his belly, dragging the dead man behind him. It was exhausting work but he kept going. When he finally stopped to rest for a moment, he realized there was almost enough room for him to stand up. The tunnel had broadened to the mouth of a cave. Mack stood up, brushed himself off, and out of habit checked his shirt pocket for a cigarette. As he stepped forward, his foot caught between two rocks, and he lost his balance and fell. He rolled on his side and reached out his right arm and leg to get up, but both limbs touched only black space, and he realized he was on the edge of a crevice. His boot had dislodged a few small rocks that tumbled over the side, and it seemed like an eternity before he heard them hit bottom. Flicking on his lighter, he examined the chasm in the dim light and guessed it to be about forty inches across. Without thinking too much about it, he grabbed the dead man by his shirt collar and shoved him into the opening. Winborne's arm caught on a jagged rock, and his body hung suspended in the crevice, dangling like a scarecrow. Mack struggled in the dark until finally he got the arm released and Winborne dropped down into the black hole. Mack couldn't see the body tumbling through the darkness but he imagined it, and fought the image of himself in Winborne's place, sailing lifelessly through the air.

There was no way to guess how deep the crevice was, but the sound when the corpse hit bottom was one he would never forget. He tore off the tweed jacket and disposed of it in the same manner. then, shaken and exhausted, he crawled back toward the cave opening.

Not all of the boards fit back into place, but there was no time to worry with it. He had to get out of there—out of town—maybe even out of the country. Hell, with $200,000 he could go any damn place he pleased.

～

Back on the main road, Mack noticed that the car's gas gauge was almost on empty. He pulled in to the next filling station and told the boy to fill it up. While the young teen was washing the windshield, Mack asked if he knew where he could get some good home cooking. Yes indeed, the boy said, he knew just the place.

"Down this here road about two miles, my cousin Essie Rose runs the Sweet Creek Cafe. Best country-fried steak and redeye gravy you ever ate. Guarantee it. Just past the old rock quarry," he said, "and get you some pie, too." Mack thanked him and gave him a $2.00 tip. He liked being a rich man.

The idea didn't come into his head until he had almost passed it by. The rock quarry. Like most abandoned quarries, it had been flooded for many years, and forgotten about by all but a few old timers who used to labor there. Mack roughly scooped the bundles of money from the briefcase and transferred them to the duffel bag. His watchful eyes darting all around him to be certain no one was around. The plain white envelope, still pressed between two rubber banded bundles, fell unnoticed into the duffel bag along with the rest of the money.

The empty briefcase was just heavy enough to hold the gas pedal down. Mack stood off to the side with his duffel bag full of cash and watched the car sail over the edge and plunge into the cold dark water.

～

"I'll have the biggest chicken fried-steak you can fit on a plate. And mashed potatoes, a couple biscuits, some fried okra, and a bucket of black coffee. Oh—and ma'am, a piece of that fine lookin' apple pie, too," he said with a smile on his face. With Winborne out of the way for good and the car at the bottom of the quarry, Mack relaxed.

"Sure thing, shug," the waitress said. The nametag on her tattered uniform read Luanne. "You need anything else, and I mean anything honey, why you just let me know." She winked and raised a penciled-on eyebrow in an attempt to flirt and then sashayed back into the kitchen. Mack laughed. Although the waitress was mildly amusing to watch as she swung her hips back and forth, and wasn't too terribly difficult to look at, he was in no way interested. Not today.

He sopped up the last bit of gravy with his biscuit and wrapped up the pie to go. Then asked Luanne if anybody in the cafe could give him a ride out of town.

"Cecil Hawkins is fixin' to leave any minute. Makin' a delivery all the way to the capital city. I'm sure he'd be obligin'. Sure do hate to see a good-lookin' fella like you run off so soon, though. Next time you come through, you stay a little while longer and I'll show you just what kinda' hospitality Sweet Creek is known for." She threw back her head, let out a gravelly laugh, and said good-bye.

V

~

BOBBY

~

1950

$\sim$

$\mathcal{M}$ack slept most of the way to Raleigh. Fatigue was part of the reason but mostly it just made it easier to avoid conversation. Cecil asked him a few questions here and there out of politeness, but he was used to traveling alone and the silence suited him just fine, too.

Once they were on the outskirts of the capital, Mack perked up and began looking out the window to spot a used-car dealer. Almost two hundred and fifty miles from Asheville seemed like a safe enough distance for him to spend a little of his money. Besides, it was possible that they wouldn't even realize Winborne was missing for a few weeks yet. Since he was the only one who knew the contents of the briefcase, there would be no suspicion of robbery, and no reason to connect him to Winborne's whereabouts.

"You can drop me here, that'd be just fine," he said. "Here's a little somethin' for yer trouble," and he handed Cecil $20. That would have been enough gas money for two trips with some left over. Cecil tipped his hat and pulled away.

Mack wandered the downtown streets until he found a small hotel, paid cash for his room, and went next door to a diner for some cornbread and Brunswick stew. He would like to have stayed in a fancier hotel, but he was still dressed in his shabby work clothes and knew he would certainly have drawn attention to himself. No, this place would just have to do until he could figure everything out. That night in his musty room, Mack did a lot of thinking. He couldn't just drive around indefinitely carrying a sack full of dough. He had to find a safe place for the money and make a new life for himself. Banks were not an option—too many questions. There was no one he could trust, and his family—his only family—was Bobby.

Maybe this was a chance for him and Bobby to start over. They could each have their own new house and live near each other. Later on when they settled down, their kids would play together and they would have a real Christmas holiday like he had always dreamed of. He picked up the phone and hurriedly dialed his brother's number. The phone rang ten or twelve times before Mack finally heard his brother's voice. "Yeah," was all the voice said.

"Bobby, is that you?" He hadn't talked to his brother in years and wasn't sure.

"Who the hell do you think it is, Babe Ruth? What'd ya want?" he said angrily.

"It's Mack. Listen, I'm comin' home. I got some real good news, Bobby. From now on everything is goin' to be okay. You don't have to worry about nothin' anymore."

"Are you drunk or just plain crazy?" Bobby snarled. "Cause I *know* I'm drunk and I *been* crazy for a long time," he laughed a sick laugh. "What the hell you talkin' about, comin' home. Comin' home to what, our childhood palace? Look, brother, you can come home and stay with me in this dump a couple of days, but don't expect no handouts. I ain't got no money and I don't need no southern comfort—except the kind that comes in a bottle."

"Don't worry, Bobby, I won't be freeloading. I'll be there in two days."

"Yeah, yeah, I can't wait," Bobby said and hung up.

Nothing could dampen Mack's spirits. Not even Bobby's cynical remarks. Once he told Bobby about the money, he would soften up, and they could learn to be a family again. But Mack had no intentions of telling Bobby exactly how much he really had. He was smarter than that.

~

The next morning was sunny and typically warm for September. The front desk clerk told Mack there was a car dealership about six blocks east toward the capitol building. He tucked the duffel bag under his arm and headed in that direction.

It was hard for him to decide which car to buy now that he could pick out any one he wanted. For that matter, he could have purchased the whole dealership and not even flinched. But a sweet little 1950 two-door Mercury convertible caught his eye. It was called a "lead sled" and was customized with fender skirts, lake pipes, and a white rolled and tucked interior. The icing on the cake was the chrome hubcaps. Why should he buy a used car when he could buy a new one with chump change? The salesman was shocked when Mack never even questioned the sticker price and paid cash on the line. He *"yes sir'd"* and *"no sir'd"* Mack and did everything but kiss his boots. Now this was the way to live. Mack pulled out of the lot and followed the signs for Highway 64 toward the coast.

He arrived in Buxton later that day and drove around to some of his favorite haunts. He was still trying to decide on a place to hide the money. Now that he was in familiar surroundings he felt like his old self again. And then it hit him. He knew the perfect place to stash the booty. Mack stopped at Wilson's Hardware and purchased a shovel, some rope, and a medium-sized metal tool box. He planned to keep $25,000 readily available and hide the rest. He would only tell Bobby about $20,000 until he decided if he could be trusted. For the last $5,000 he had something special in mind.

The following day he called Bobby and was surprised when his brother answered the phone on the second ring, sounding sober. "Bobby, I'm in town. I got a lot to tell ya."

"What makes you think I care? Are you comin' or not? Don't you think I ain't got nothing better to do than wait for your sorry ass to show up?" He was even more hostile when he was sober. And his cruel comments brought back painful memories of the tauntings that led to bloody fistfights when they were younger. Mack was never able to overcome his younger brother's greater physical prowess. Even though he was several years older, Bobby had grown taller and stronger than he early in their teens and took great pleasure in bullying his older brother. Mack liked to think he was at least smarter than Bobby, even if he was weaker. But in his heart he knew that if his brother sobered up, Bobby would come out on top in the brains department as well.

"Listen, could you meet me at the old lighthouse?" Mack said.

"What for?"

"I can't tell you anything else over the phone. Just meet me at the old place where we used to play when we was kids. Say, in about thirty minutes."

"This better be good, big brother. Cause if you're playin' games with me I'll have to teach your scrawny ass a lesson. O.K. thirty minutes." And he slammed the phone down.

Mack lit up a Lucky and was relieved he had already hidden the bulk of the money. It might take a couple of years for Bobby to come around. And if he didn't, Mack was prepared to take his remaining stash and disappear from the Outer Banks for good.

The old lighthouse looked about the same. He had always loved it there. Too bad it was closed down in 1936. Since then, it had been in a steadily declining state of disrepair. Bobby and Mack had spent many hours playing in the dunes and watching for ships that dared to navigate Diamond Shoals. Those were good times—before their mother left and before Bobby's dark nature surfaced.

Mack climbed to the top and waited for Bobby. The view from two hundred feet up was spectacular. The coastline disappeared into the horizon on one side, and on the other he could see the cape. He thought he loved the mountains, but now, gazing out over the glistening ocean and watching the crashing breakers, he was glad to be back home. Feeling reborn, he decided he would donate some of his money to paint the lighthouse and repair the rusted ironwork that distinguished it from all the rest. If the old lanterns were replaced with new electric ones, then maybe it could be used again to guide ships along this treacherous region of the North Carolina coast.

Mack had always wanted respect. The kind he saw Mr. Winborne receive. Not just for being rich, but for being a decent man. The lighthouse donation was a good start, he decided. It was too bad about the old man's accident, but at least Mack could put some of his money to good use and ease a little of his guilt for running off with it.

When Bobby showed up, he was in as foul a mood in person as he had been on the phone. Mack could hear him cursing as he stomped on the 268th and final step. No hello, no how are you, how ya doing. Nothing. Same old Bobby.

"Goddamn, Mack, you better tell me something that's gonna give me a hard-on draggin' my ass all the way to the top of this lighthouse." He was breathing hard and sweating. Mack thought momentarily of the fat little groundskeeper on the Winborne estate. Bobby was unshaven and dirty, and Mack was suprised how much older he looked than his years.

"Bobby, I been workin' up in the mountains over the last few months. Up near Asheville. A really fine gentleman give me a job and I done real well."

"So what? What are you ramblin' about? I swear Mack, you better have a point to this story, or . . . " Bobby threatened.

"Hold on. Hold on. See, this gentleman was rich—I mean, real rich." Bobby was listening now. "And, well, come the end of summer, he sort of had a bad accident and won't be hiring anybody ever again, if you know what I mean. Anyhow, he left me a little bonus cause I was such a good employee."

Bobby was definitely interested now, but not in all the stupid little details of Mack's job, just the part about the bonus.

"What sort of bonus?"

"Hold yer horses,now. See, Mr. Winborne took a liking to me 'cause I saved his life once. So he left me some money. I guess it was his way of sayin' 'thank you.'"

"God dammit, Mack—how much?"

"A lot, Bobby, a real lot. Enough for us to start over and have a real good life. You don't ever have to worry about nothin' ever again. I got some of it on me and the rest I put away in a safe place." *Oh, Lord.* In his excitement, Mack let slip that he had stashed some of the money elsewhere. Bobby always made him so nervous—he could always tell when Mack was hiding something from him. "And you deserve some of it, too," Mack said.

Bobby looked at him and spoke so quietly it was almost a whisper. "How much money you got on you, Mack?"

"Twenty thousand. Cash. It's for both of us. We can start over, Bobby."

Bobby's mouth was gaping open in disbelief. He looked at Mack and said in a low voice, "Are you tellin' me—that you have—$20,000 U.S. dollars in cash, free and clear?"

"I am, brother."

"And—you got more hid somewhere else?"

"Yup, I ain't lyin'."

Bobby started laughing hysterically. Tears ran down his face and he clutched at the iron railing surrounding the narrow lightkeeper's walk. Mack started to laugh with him, thinking perhaps this was the start of a new relationship with his troubled brother. He leaned over to help Bobby steady himself, and they were still laughing. Bobby draped his arm around his older brother, and for a split second, Mack saw a glimpse of the little brother he had once known in Bobby's blue eyes.

Bobby let out a long sigh and said, "Well, I guess I won't beat your butt after all." He smiled and continued, "So, big brother, how much more is there? Hmmm? You gonna tell me where all this loot is, or do I have to guess?"

"Like I said, I got the 20k on me. But don't worry, Bobby, the rest of it's in a real safe place. You know, 'til we figure out what we're doin'," he said.

"Maybe you didn't hear me. I said, *how much* more? *Where* is it!" His expression had hardened and his eyes held Mack in an icy glare.

Mack started to explain, but Bobby wasn't interested in long explanations. He grabbed Mack by the collar and started shaking him. He was yelling now and shoving him up against the railing. Everything was happening so fast. Mack couldn't think. The veins in Bobby's face and neck were popping out, and he kept screaming where was the money. He pushed Mack further over the railing and threatened to drop him over the side if he didn't give up the location.

Mack was in a panic. He was so close to his dream. His luck had been so good until now, and Bobby was about to take it all away from him. What good would his money be if he was dead?

"O.K., O.K., Bobby—I'll tell you. I'll tell you. Just back off."

"Not until you say where it is. Right now!" He dangled Mack a little further over the edge.

"O.K., just calm down. I hid the money . . . " he started to say, then stopped as they heard a moaning sound and then a crack. A four-foot section of railing pulled up and out of its rusted fastenings and gave way under their weight. Bobby released Mack and grabbed for a dangling section of the metal railing and hung precariously 200 feet above the sandy beach.

But it was too late for Mack. He stared up at Bobby in a tailspin of disbelief and horror—and fell to his death.

Bobby pulled himself back up onto the platform, staggered to his feet, and then raced down the stairs. Mack's twisted body was lying at the base of the granite foundation of the lighthouse. A few beach-combers were running in that direction to see what had happened. He shook his brother for signs of life. There were none. Then he deftly searched his pockets and found an envelope of cash. "I'll be damned, the bastard wasn't lying," Bobby said as he stuffed the bills in his pocket. "And you were right, big brother, I do deserve this money," and mockingly patted the top of Mack's head.

When the police arrived, Bobby told them that he and Mack had met at the lighthouse to have a family reunion of sorts. That they were real close and hadn't seen each other for a while and wanted to catch up like brothers often do. The dangling railing was proof enough for the police that it was an accident. They asked him a few more questions and then offered their condolences.

Bobby went back to his trailer in tears.

Tears of joy.

~

*M*arguerite ran across the lawn from the manor house toward the greenhouse, with her arms outstretched, carrying a small package. It was wrapped in plain brown paper and was addressed to Josè Rodriguez. She ran in to the greenhouse and excitedly announced to Josè that he had a delivery. It was rare that any of the servants received packages. Especially Josè. Letters arrived regularly, but most of the servants came from humble beginnings and, save for an occasional birthday present or Christmas token, there were very few packages. In twenty-five years, Josè had received only one other package. After his father died, his wife lovingly sent him a few of his father's personal belongings, since he was unable to return to Mexico for his burial. He hoped this package did not contain similar contents.

Marguerite handed him the package and waited eagerly to see what was in it. However, she could see that he was uncomfortable in her presence and kindly slipped out. Josè unwrapped the package and stared at the contents, perplexed. Underneath the brown wrapping was a carton of Lucky Strike cigarettes, $5,000 in cash, and a note that said, "Well amigo, looks like my horse finally came in. Good luck. M."

Josè smiled a grateful smile. He was finally going home. In 1950, five thousand dollars was a lot of money. In Mexico, it would be a fortune.

~

VI

~

DEVON

~

1990

$\mathcal{H}$is world was certainly a far cry from her own. Devon had no idea where she was, other than in the memory of a man dead for nearly forty years. She was at the bottom of a split staircase in a magnificent Tudor mansion. The house appeared to be empty, or at least the overall silence led her to believe that. She looked around at the exquisite furnishings and period furniture and thought of Milly. For some odd reason the clarity of her vision came in and out of focus intermittently, making some objects crystal clear and others barely recognizable. She tried to adjust as best she could and take in as much of the surroundings as possible.

In her "waking dreams," Devon was usually able to move from point A to point B, instantly, by just thinking about it. In this dream she was less in control of her movements but still able to maneuver adequately. She floated up the marble staircase and paused at the top, then looked down the long hallway that ran in opposite directions on either side of her. Her physical body did not seem to be present, but she was nevertheless equipped with her five senses.

What was she here for? And what was it she was supposed to see? Was this where the man committed suicide? She heard footsteps padding softly down the carpeted hallway toward her. A gentleman in a tweed jacket and sharply creased trousers moved closer. Perhaps, it was the man whose face she was recreating on her work table. She looked at his face to compare it to the bust by memory, but then her vision blurred, and his features went fuzzy like the protected witnesses she'd seen on court TV. It was impossible to tell what he looked like other than he was Caucasian. When her vision cleared again, he had moved past her. It seemed every time she moved around to look at his face, he either turned the other way or her eyesight went out of focus. This was the weirdest and most frustrating dream she had ever experienced, and it was clear she had little control of the situation.

One thing she did notice was the spring in his step and his relaxed posture. This was not the tragic demeanor she would have expected of a suicide victim. As she watched, he stopped a moment, pulled out a silver pocket watch, and checked the time. She was hovering over his shoulder now. The numbers were too small to read, but as he snapped the watch case closed, she could see his fingers rubbing back and forth over it. A well established habit. She strained to see the initials engraved on it. It looked like a B.L. or F.L. perhaps, with the third letter obscured by his thumb. She didn't think these were the same initials Detective Whyte told her about. She couldn't remember.

He continued down the hall but slowed his pace when he approached the doorway of the room at the top of the stairs, then halted. Following, Devon saw that he was observing a poorly dressed young man standing behind a desk in the mahogany paneled office. For a moment both men were motionless, the younger still oblivious to the older one's presence. Faces almost coming into focus and then out again. Devon was confused. Where did the suicide fit in? She wished she could ask them some questions.

Suddenly, the older man withdrew and scrambled back down the hall a short distance, slipping into a room on his right. When he reappeared, he was carrying a gun.

Devon knew what must be coming next and tried desperately to escape her vision, but the dreams didn't work like that. She was meant to be a part of this, for reasons unknown to her. She tried to close her eyes, but in the dream world there is no such thing. The mind's eye is always open.

The man in the tweed jacket returned and steadied himself in the doorway. As he reached his arms up and positioned the shotgun on his left shoulder, he dislodged a linen handkerchief from his jacket pocket, and it fell to the floor. Devon glided over to the square of fabric and saw that three initials, most likely the same as on the silver pocket watch, were embroidered in fancy black letters. The first two letters were not B, or L, as she thought on the watch, but maybe a C, and T, and the third maybe an N or M. She just couldn't be sure. He was standing almost on top of the handkerchief and the folds in the linen distorted the monogram.

Distracted by the kerchief, Devon suddenly realized an argument was under way. The voices were muffled, and she was frustrated that she could not understand what was being said. It was as though they were underwater. She could hear them, but could not understand them.

The men started to wrestle and grapple with the gun. She tried to scream but nothing came out. The gun dropped to the floor, and in the next instant the two men were tumbling through the doorway. Devon looked around for someone to help but the three of them were alone. The next thing she saw was the older man sailing over the top step, grabbing wildly at the air in an attempt to abort his fall. As he fell backward, he seemed to look right at her, and, for only an instant, she saw his eyes.

He cracked his head on the fifth step. She automatically counted the rest of the steps as his body rolled down the staircase and finally came to rest in a mangled heap of arms and legs at the bottom. Twenty five steps in all. "How odd," she thought absently, "the same number of steps as my apartment."

If this was her man, then the fractured C2 had occurred on the fifth marble step. What was not clear to Devon was whether the whole thing had been an accident or as Detective Whyte had secretly suspected and tried to hide from her, homicide. She had been so intent on deciphering the initials on the handkerchief, that she missed the crucial moment that would have revealed the truth. It was quite possible the young man had pushed the older one down the steps. If only she could have heard what the argument was about.

An instant later, the house was quiet again. Devon was unable to see where the young man had disappeared, and she had no idea what to do next. There was no sign of either man, no blood, no evidence whatsoever that anything had just transpired. Everything happened so fast, and now it looked as though nothing had ever happened at all. Did she really see something or was it a dream within a dream? She was confused, desperate to escape that hideous scene, and feeling nothing except helplessness.

Yanked from the dream as abruptly as she was thrust into it, Devon dropped her hands from the sculpture, and collapsed beneath it onto the work table. The hazel eyes looked straight ahead with a lifeless, glassy stare. Shaken, she reached over and blindly grabbed at the plastic sheeting on the work table. Careful not to look up, she covered the clay face and ran out of the museum.

"Milly" was the only clear thought she had.

*A*t the apartment building, Devon pounded on her neighbor's door. "Milly—Milly, please answer the door!" The light was on but no one answered. She pounded again. A few tears trickled down her cheeks and spattered on her blouse. "Milly, are you in there? I need to talk to you." Silence. Not home. She vaguely remembered Milly telling her something about the National Opera Company being on tour in Raleigh, and that tonight was opening night for *La Traviata*, Milly's favorite. She had told Devon she had a front-row seat and would probably be out late, and that Devon shouldn't worry. Devon wiped her eyes and scolded herself for overreacting, calming herself down by doing so. She blew her nose, and reluctantly turned to her own apartment door, fumbling with the key. She would have to wait until tomorrow to talk with her friend.

Wearily, Devon poured herself a glass of red wine and sank into a hot bath. It was almost impossible to block out the evening's unnerving scenario. She hoped Milly would help her make sense of it all in the morning.

9:00 A.M. "Nathan, I can't come in to work today. I don't feel well at all." It wasn't really a lie. She didn't say she was sick—she said she didn't feel well. And she didn't.

"O.K., Devon, the joke's over. The first couple of times it was funny, but not any more. You know we have way too much going on at the museum today, and I don't have time for games," he said in a serious tone.

"I'm not playing games. I was working late last night and suddenly got ill. S-sorry, Nathan, I'll make it up to you. See you on Monday, I promise." There was no way she was going to the museum until she had talked with Milly and figured out what to do.

"This is really bad timing. But I guess if you're sick, you're sick. All right, see you first thing on Monday. And try not to have anything else happen between now and then, huh?"

If only he knew what she had been through the night before, he would have canned that last comment.

Although she was no longer agitated, the image of Mr. "X," lying at the bottom of the stairs kept popping up in her mind. How could she possibly finish the sculpt now? There was no way she could put her hands on that skull again. It was too risky. She was already more involved than she wanted to be. The worst part would be delivering the bad news to Detective Whyte that she was quitting the project. He and everyone else would be so disappointed in her, and all with good reason. She despised herself for being so spineless. It had started out so well but because of her fear the project was coming to a screeching halt. Prior to last night she had needed reassurance, but this morning she needed advice and a way out.

Devon felt like she was a hundred years old as she made her way toward the door to see if Milly was up yet. But before she turned the knob, she stepped on an envelope that had been slipped underneath her door. She opened it and read the familiar handwriting.

"Dev—gone to doctor's. Think I'm coming down with the flu. I'll stop by later. Love, Milly."

She rubbed her puffy eyelids and brushed her hair back from her face. This was the third time this year Milly had buckled under the flu bug.

By noon Devon had still not heard from or seen Milly, and she was starting to get concerned. She was pacing around her apartment, when she heard keys rattling in the hallway outside her door. "Thank God—she's home."

Milly looked tired, but when Devon asked her about the visit to the doctor, she sidestepped the details and said she was just a little under the weather, had already picked up a prescription, and would be fine. Nothing to worry about. Devon asked if they could talk.

At first Milly was fascinated with Devon's dreams and perked up as they began to patch together the symbolism of the dream world with the real world. They surmised that the endless stairs were a metaphor for Devon's mounting stress level of late, mixed in with the resurfacing of her peculiar habit of counting steps. And the intermittent flashing light was just the security guard's flashlight. They were both quite satisfied with their evaluation of the first episode. It made perfect sense and Devon relaxed a little.

Devon then began recounting the events of the waking dream at the mansion. She described the elegant furnishings, the plush oriental rugs, the portrait filled walls, the works of art, and finally the double staircase with the pink marble steps. Milly's entire posture and facial expression began to change. No longer listening with mere curiosity, she became serious and contemplative.

Finally, when Devon got to the part about the two men, Milly interrupted her for the first time.

"What did the fellow in the tweed jacket look like?"

"I can't say, exactly, his features were fuzzy. Although—I think he was older by the way he moved—and just for a second, I did see his eyes. Hazel colored. That I know for sure."

"Hmm. You said something about the way he walked?" Milly questioned.

"Well, yeah. He sort of had a little spring in his step, you know?" Devon was clueless as to where Milly was going with this.

"Could it have been a limp?"

"I . . . guess so. But it was so slight—barely noticeable. Why? What are you thinking, Mil?" Devon asked.

"Forget it. Just a thought. Now, you couldn't see the letters on the silver watch, and you say the initials on the hankie didn't match up with the initials the detective told you about, right?"

"Right. Well, I'm pretty sure—I couldn't remember the letters." Devon scrunched up her face and looked perplexed, "Anyway, I think I remember Detective Whyte telling me that the watch they found with the skeletal remains was gold and the guy in the dream wore a silver one. The more I think about this the less sense it makes. If this wasn't the same man, then who was he?" Devon was thinking out loud.

Devon and Milly sat there without saying a word for several minutes. Both of them going in opposite directions with their thoughts. Devon rambled on.

"You know what, Mil? I'm ashamed to admit it, but I'm relieved that at least the recurring dream about falling was a premonition for that poor man and not me!" she shivered. Milly's attention was still somewhere else and she wasn't listening. Devon misread her distraction for fatigue and started to get up, "I better get going, Milly. Hope you feel better. I'll give you a call later, okay? "

"Yes, of course, Luv,—we'll talk later." Milly smiled and seemed to be back to her usual self.

In her apartment, Devon picked at the chicken leg that she took out of the fridge for lunch. She kept going over things in her head while she pulled stringy little pieces of meat off the bone. The initials that didn't match, the silver watch, the look of terror in the man's eyes as he fell. She thought about his head striking the stairs and her hand jerked in a spastic twitch, which sent the drumstick flying from her greasy fingers over the plate and sliding across the table. Devon laughed at herself and the absurdity of the moment, and then reached to pick up the straggly chicken leg. She brought it close to her face and stared at a dark spot along the middle of the bone. A small crack had allowed the marrow to seep out of the bone during cooking and discolored it. Almost instantly Devon made the connection between the drumstick, the pathology report, and something Milly had said.

"It is possible that the fracture healed with slight angulation or distortion of the bone and would have resulted in a minimal alteration in appearance and function of the leg."

And then Milly's question, *"Could it have been a limp?"* Devon darted over to the telephone and dialed Detective Whyte's office. She wondered about something else.

"Hello, Devon. What can I do for you?" He asked in an apparently good mood.

"I was thinking about the watch that was found with the body. Did you say it was gold?"

"Yes. Why?" He said.

"Oh . . . okay. Never mind. I thought for some reason it might have been silver," she answered, disappointed. She was going nowhere again.

"Well, it could easily have been mistaken for silver. It's white gold. Real popular back then. Everything, going okay?" he asked trying to get her to reveal something. Now the "silver" watch made sense, she thought. "Fine, fine. Thanks. Sorry for the bother. I'd better let you get back to work, now," she said. "Oh, one last thing," she added quickly, hoping she could pull it off, "where did you say the body was found?"

"I didn't," he retorted.

She felt really stupid. Who did she think she was talking to, Barney Fife?

"Why do you want to know? Got a hot lead?" he teased.

"No, just curious."

"If it helps, we found him at the bottom of a mine shaft. What'd you think, Devon? A jumper, an accident—maybe homicide?" He was purposefully making her uncomfortable and she guessed it was to put her in her place.

Milly was sitting in her favorite chair stroking Gabby, her plump, ill-mannered cat, when Devon showed back up an hour or so later to see how she was.

"Feeling much better, luv. Thanks. It's amazing what a little cat nap can do for you," she smiled as Gabby nestled deeper into her lap.

Devon returned the smile and was glad to see Milly in a better mood. "By the way, I think it could definitely have been a limp." Her thoughts came spilling out.

"Pardon, me?" Milly asked as she looked up at Devon.

"I remembered a paragraph in the M.E.'s report that mentioned a fracture in one leg that could have altered his movement. The fracture was insignificant for the most part, but it could have affected the way he walked. A slight limp. And the watch was white gold— looks just like silver." Devon came up for air.

"White gold? Are you sure?" Milly questioned.

"Uh-huh. Spoke to Dectective Whyte. Dammit, if only I was able to match up the initials then I would be sure the man in the dream was the same guy I was trying to find a face for. I know he didn't kill himself, but whether or not he was pushed . . ." Devon trailed off.

"What do you mean "was" the guy you were finding a face for? Are you quitting?"

"I have to. I can't—I mean, I don't want to touch that skull again. It's too much for me, Milly. If there was some other way to help, I would. I'll call and tell the police that it wasn't a suicide—for all that's worth, but they'll just think I'm crazy." Devon couldn't look her in the eyes. Milly took Devon's hand in hers and Devon felt compelled to look up.

"Would you do it for me? If I asked you to?" Milly's voice was barely a whisper.

"Of . . . of course—but why do you care so much about—" she was cut short.

"Then I'm asking you to finish it for me," in an even stranger tone.

"But—I don't underst—"

Milly interrupted again. "Shhh. Don't ask me any questions, right now. Just finish the sculpt and let me see it when it's complete. *If* I'm right, I'll explain everything then. If not, it won't matter anyway, and you'll have accomplished something for yourself at the very least." She waited for Devon's answer.

At this point, Devon was more concerned about the look on Milly's face than she was about the prospect of touching the skull again and quickly told Milly what she wanted to hear. "Sure, Milly. You know I would do anything you asked of me. I'll . . .get back on it right away and we'll go down and look at it together. Okay? It shouldn't take me much longer."

"Thank you, Devon," was all she said.

The previous night, when Devon had panicked, she had no clue what to do or what her next move should be. She thought Milly would have all the answers and would be her fountain of wisdom. But now, seeing her friend in such an agitated state, Devon knew that she had to be strong and act accordingly. Milly was counting on her.

Devon slipped back into the artist's studio later that afternoon just before closing. Nathan was surprised to see her but said nothing. She had been acting so weird the past week and was preoccupied to the degree that she barely said hello to anyone, that he decided she must be having "female" problems and just left her alone.

She approached the bust and checked her measurements again, focused her concentration, and began working. Her hands manipulated the clay and, thankfully, there was never even a tremor to coax her back into his world. Maybe it was because she was so focused on finishing that she subconsciously would not allow it.

She made a few last adjustments on the tissue around the eyes so that the lids appeared soft and relaxed and added a few more lines around the mouth to better reflect his age. If she had been able to clearly see the features of the man in the dream, she could have compared it to the face in front of her. She dismissed the thought—the bones were always right. She must let the bones guide her hands—not her imagination.

The armature was built so that she could continue to sculpt the clay down the neck and over the shoulders, stopping at the upper arms. When she was satisfied with the way it looked, she added a wig and clothing. She chose a white shirt and paisley tie. The wig was cut short and had some graying at the temples. The face before her was finally complete. She had finished it in less than four hours.

Tomorrow, she and Milly would look at her work together and she would find out what was going on.

~

They stood in front of the work table in silence, holding private their fears. It was Milly that spoke first.

"Devon, before we take a look at this fellow, would you mind verifying one thing for me? I'd like to know what the initials were that Detective Whyte found."

"No problem. I have them written here in my journal." Devon went to her drawer and took out the notebook without question. She thumbed through it until she found what she was looking for. "Here it is. They could only make out the first two initials—E.J.—blank. Wow, I was way off . . ." Devon tried to lighten up the mood a little and then stopped mid sentence when she saw her friend's face. "Mil, what's wrong? Are you ill? What is it?" Devon was frightened. Milly just stared ahead and didn't utter a sound. She was a grayish, sickly color. "Milly?"

"I'm all right, " Milly said at last, "I think I know who this man was. Take off the sheeting and let me see his face."

Devon did as she was told and slowly pulled the drape from the bust. A small guttural sound escaped from Milly's lips and she sank into the chair in front of the table. There was no mistaking this man for anyone other than her uncle.

Milly cleared her throat and said. "I just can't believe it could be possible after all these years. We had given up so long ago, . . ." and trailed off.

"Milly, for God's sake, what are you talking about? Who—Who was he?" Devon pressed.

"His name was Edmon James Winborne. He was my uncle." Milly drew in a labored breath and began. "When I was about eighteen years old, Uncle Edmon disappeared. He was a very wealthy man and prone to certain eccentricities, one of them being spontaneous trips that to this day remain unexplained. On these peculiar outings, he preferred to drive the car himself rather than his chauffeur, and usually returned to the mansion in a week or so. In the autumn of 1950, he set out on one of these mysterious junkets, destination unknown. But this time he never returned. Never sent word to the servants, no note, nothing. It was like he disappeared off the face of the earth." Milly looked up at Devon; the pain in her eyes was obvious. "He was my mother's youngest brother." She tried to control the wavering in her voice. "There was a lengthy investigation that went on for months, but nothing was ever found. Our family hired private investigators to supplement the police work but still nothing turned up."

"Go on, Mil." Devon couldn't believe what she was hearing.

"Eventually, we gave up hope of ever finding him, and after seven years his estate was released from probate. I learned that I was the beneficiary of the bulk of his fortune. He was a good man, Devon. Very generous. He left a good portion to charities. I kept a bit of money in a trust for the future, and I live off the interest. I took home some pieces of his furniture and gave the rest to charities, museums, and such. At twenty-five years old, that much money was an overwhelming burden for me." Milly sat back in the chair and took another deep breath.

"Oh god, I don't know what to say—I'm so sorry for you to find out like this," Devon said sympathetically. Poor Milly. It must have been crushing to come to this realization in such an unexpected manner. Devon handed her friend some tissues. After a few minutes Milly seemed to come back around and the color returned to her cheeks.

"I'm sorry I scared you. Even though I suspected—the reality of this was quite a shock," Milly admitted. "Devon, you really did do a remarkable job."

"Thanks—I think. What was it that gave you the inkling it might be your uncle—if you don't mind my asking?" Devon was embarrassed but asked anyway.

Milly sniffed and then answered. "I don't mind. In fact, I want to talk about it. The first thing was the pink marble staircase, and the way you described the mansion was uncanny. Then—when you said he walked funny, the silver pocket watch, the hazel eyes—I started to wonder. I think I knew. The initials—well, that was the icing on the cake. And now, sitting here looking at his face, there is no question. It's Edmon."

"Milly, I'm as shocked as you are with how this whole thing has turned out," Devon said. Winborne's face poised and now seemingly peaceful only made Devon more uncomfortable about the loose ends regarding his death. "Did anyone talk to him on the day of his disappearance?" Devon asked.

"No. But one of the groundsmen saw him drive away and that was the last anyone ever saw of him. Neither his car nor his body was ever found." Milly sighed. "Well, at least it's over."

Devon reached over and put her arm around Milly. "Is it?" Devon asked.

"What do you mean?" Milly looked puzzled.

Devon was already thinking ahead. "Milly, listen, I have an idea. I'll call Detective Whyte first thing Monday and tell him what I know. I suppose he'll need to talk with you and get some sort of proof. But once he starts to investigate your uncle's disappearance, he'll see we're right. Maybe if I go back into the vision there will be more answers as to whether it was an accidental death or . . . you know . . . homicide. As soon as I have all the pieces put together, I'll fill you in."

"How do you know you can do that; go back into the dream?" Milly asked.

"I don't—but it's worth a try. We have to find out what really happened to him." She kissed Milly on the forehead and noticed that her skin felt feverish. "Now, let's get back home. You need to take it easy today—and try to get some rest."

Devon suddenly felt strong and was undaunted by either the prospect of Detective Whyte's probable ridicule, or the thought of voluntarily reentering Winborne's death memory. She felt incredibly protective of Milly, and she likened herself to the proverbial "mother bear." For the first time in their five-year relationship, it was Milly who needed Devon. And Devon would die before she would ever let her friend down.

On Monday morning, Devon walked into the studio at about 7:15, anxious to find out if she could willingly reenter the dream and bring closure to Milly and herself. Swallowing her fear, she closed her eyes and began some deep breathing and then cleared her mind of as much as possible.

When she felt completely relaxed, she took one more deep breath, and placed her hands on the sculpt. She tried to visualize the mansion as she had seen it the first time. Devon had never attempted to initiate a dream before, and she was surprised how easy it was for her to flash back into Winborne's death memory again. She was even more surprised at how calm she was. This time, as she watched the scene play itself out, she focused carefully on the two men struggling with the gun. As they tumbled toward the stairs, she could see everything she had missed the first time. The younger man's grip on Winborne broke loose when his foot caught in the railing. Winborne had nothing to grab on to and the inertia created during the brawl made it impossible for him to stop himself from going over the top step. His death was unequivocally accidental.

Although she was able to reenter the vision, she was able to re-main there only for a few minutes. Long enough to replay what she had seen earlier but not long enough to learn anything more about the young man who was with him. She was hoping she could follow the young man out of the manor house to see what happened next, but when she floated toward the door, the dream ended and she was snapped back to reality. After that, no matter how hard she tried to return to the vision, she could not. Her purpose for being there was finished.

At 8:30, he received the call. Detective Whyte was smiling the whole time he was talking to Devon on the phone. "Artists," he thought, "they're all a bunch of kooks, and now she thinks she's a detective." But he jotted down the name and the date anyhow. He was going to give her a little grief about her "hocus-pocus" theory of who this man was, but for some reason he changed his mind. She sounded different today. Not the nervous Nelly he had met a week ago. Today her voice was strong, articulate, and to the point. She matter-of-factly gave him the information and told him the bust would be ready to be photographed on Tuesday.

He was impressed—she had finished it early. But what was her rush? He began going through his files on missing persons dating back to September 1950. The computer indicated there had been, in fact, an Edmon James Winborne, renowned businessman and philan-thropist, reported missing on September 21, 1950, three weeks after he was last seen. He pulled up the rest of the file and had hard copies printed out. Among the reports were newspaper articles and family photos of a distinguished-looking man. He was intrigued. Now, if the photos matched the face on Devon's reconstruction, the case would be closed, and no doubt he would gain a lot of recognition for solving such a tough one with such progressive methods as forensic facial reconstruction. He would be the talk of the department. All he had to do was gather positive ID information from the supposed neice—and it was all locked up.

"I better think about getting a new suit for the commissioner's commendation and the press photos," he said confidently, as he picked a microscopic fleck of lint off his sleeve.

"Do you have any news for me?" Milly asked her friend on the other end of the phone.

"It was an accident. No question. I saw the whole thing all over again, and the young man didn't deliberately push your uncle. They both just lost their balance, and unfortunately Edmon was closest to the top step. I'm sorry, Mil."

Milly paused and then said, "Thank you, Devon. I know it wasn't easy for you to witness it a second time. I'm grateful. At least now I can put this to rest."

The odd thing was, it really hadn't been that difficult for Devon to witness it a second time. "Anything else I can do for you, Mil? Are you feeling any better?" Devon asked.

"No, you've done plenty. I'm feeling better, dear. Really."

"Oh . . . Milly, do you have any idea at all who the young man might have been? I saw his face and he was nice looking—kind of scruffy—but he had a kind face."

"I've been thinking about him, too. Absolutely no idea who he might have been. But Uncle Edmon had dealings with people from every walk of life. It could have been anyone." Milly answered with slight exasperation.

They said good-bye and Devon went to the lounge and poured herself a cup of coffee. She sat at the table dotting the powder sugar crumbs from her doughnut with her fingers and licking them. She wondered why she felt so uneasy. With most of the questions regarding Edmon's death answered, she should have felt satisfied. Instead there was a knot in the pit of her stomach. She got the feeling Milly wasn't telling her everything. And if she did know something, why would she keep it from her? Devon topped off the second cup of coffee and returned to her desk to dive into the stack of papers that Nathan had asked her to read over. Every few minutes she had to remind herself to keep her attention on what she was doing. She could not shake off the feeling that something still wasn't quite right.

~

*T*he headline read, "**FACE FINDER RAISES DEAD MAN FROM THE GRAVE.**" The front page of the newspaper included a lengthy article on the events that led up to Edmon Winborne's identification. There were also side-by-side full-color photos of the forensic reconstruction and Milly's uncle. The resemblance between the photo and the sculpt was so close that one might have thought Devon had looked at the photo while working on his face. On page 5A the story continued, with photos of Devon in her studio. Detective Whyte was mentioned briefly. He was quite peeved that the reporter practically ignored him and didn't even ask him to be photographed. He handed Devon her check for $1,800 and told her he would call her again if the opportunity ever arose. She hoped not.

The museum received numerous congratulatory phone calls and one very important letter from a patron who wished to make a substantial contribution to the art department to further their work in that area. Nathan announced that he was pleased and, despite his earlier lecture regarding her absenteeism, he told Devon to take a few days off—she had earned it.

~

$\mathcal{T}$here it was. The most beautiful thing she had laid eyes on in weeks. Ready and waiting for her and her alone. Her old friend. Her blue Chevy. Eddie raised the hood and pointed to each and every new part on her rebuilt engine. Said it was as good as new, except for the scabby rust spots along the doors and under the bumpers. Eddie was as happy to get his check as Devon was to get her car. He handed her the keys and reminded her to take better care of her car from now on.

"Don't worry, Eddie. I've learned that lesson twice over. No offense, but I hope I never have to see you again," she said with a smile. She cruised to her apartment with the windows rolled down and the radio off so she could listen to the sound of her engine purring. Donny gave her a double-tall cappuccino on the house and told her how nice it was to see her back in the neighborhood. She smiled to herself and thought how good it was to be in control again.

~

$\mathcal{T}$he invitation delivered five weeks later, was handwritten on fine stationery and addressed to Devon.

Dear Miss Gardiner,

In recognition of your most generous contribution of $100,000.00,
The Lighthouse Preservation Society of N.C. requests your presence
for a reception in your honor on November 8, 1990, at 7:00 P.M. at
the Historic Palmer House. Accommodations will be provided for
you and your co-contributor, Miss Milly Bradshaw.

Respectfully yours,

R.S.V.P.   *Emily Carson, Chairperson*

Devon read it over three times before the words made any sense. Contribution? Lighthouse Society? $100,000? The only letters she was familiar with were MILLY.

"Come on in, Devon. I've been expecting you." Milly was laughing and holding her own invitation in her hand when she answered the door. "Sit down and just listen. Do you think you can do that?" Devon nodded and obeyed. Milly struggled for a moment to find the right words, and then she began.

"Some of my favorite childhood memories are the family trips we took to the beach. Before my parents died, Uncle Edmon, Aunt Danielle and my family would pile into the car with everything we could think of and drive down to the Outer Banks. We did this at least two or three times a year. Everyone had so much fun. We would have midnight picnics on the beach, go fishing, and walk for miles up and down the strand.

Uncle Edmon would tell stories about the lighthouse keepers and how dangerous their jobs could be during foul weather. Before being converted to electricity, the lighthouses were lit with huge oil lanterns that needed constant attention and refilling throughout the night. It was a difficult and lonely life. But despite all that the lightkeepers usually kept their jobs until they died, and often the position was then passed down to their wives or children. Milly filled two cups with tea and continued.

"Anyway, he admired their dedication and I think he almost felt personally indebted to them for the safe passage of our ancestors who emigrated from Europe. He told the same story over and over of how our family first came to America," she laughed, "but no one complained. He was so proud to be an American. He never forgot where he came from. In fact, he took those trips to the coast to remind himself that if it weren't for the courage of his grandparents crossing such treacherous waters, he would never have been given the opportunities that he was blessed with." Devon finished her tea; her eyes fixed on Milly.

"What I'm getting at is—I made the contribution to the Lighthouse Society in his memory. He would have liked the idea of donating his money to an organization that preserves the lighthouses. Thanks to you, Devon, my uncle is finally laid to rest in peace, and that's why your name joined mine as a co-contributor." Milly smiled and waited for Devon's reaction.

"Milly, I'm so flattered. But, my god, $100,000?" Devon stuttered.

"I know, I know—just listen," Milly scolded. "I know it sounds like an incredible amount of money, but my uncle was *quite* wealthy. And $100,000 won't go as far as you think with the amount of work that needs to be done to repair some of the lighthouses. I told you I kept a bit of money for myself after his estate disbursement, and I still have enough to last me the rest of my life. I don't require much, anyhow, you know that."

"Wow! I guess your idea of a 'bit' of money and my idea of a 'bit' of money are just a wee bit different!" Devon smiled. "I had a feeling you were hiding something from me."

Milly chuckled and told Devon she was looking forward to the trip to the coast for the reception. Devon agreed and suggested they both go shopping for new dresses since they were being honored by the high-society crowd. With their lives seemingly back on track, the two women celebrated with a ceremonial cup of Earl Grey and toasted to their illustrious friendship and many years of good health and happiness.

VII

~

DEVON

~

1990

$\mathcal{T}$he following weeks passed fairly quickly as the hubbub over Winborne's case began to die down. Devon had received a lot of attention from the newspaper article at first, but now it was back to the same old grind. She hadn't yet received an invitation from Joan Lunden or Oprah to be on their shows, and it was now apparent she wasn't going to. Every time Nathan walked by her desk, he smiled and winked at her, but she hadn't heard word one about a salary increase. She tried to be big about the whole thing but her financial situation was getting tighter and tighter, and lately, she had started to consider a part-time job to supplement her income.

The few hundred dollars that Devon had left from the forensic reconstruction were spent on charge card bills and miscellaneous expenses. Financially, she was back to square one. At times like this, it was hard for her to understand how Milly could have so much money and not care about it. All Devon ever dreamed of was a *little* financial freedom. And while she admired the generous donation to the Lighthouse Society, she couldn't help wishing Milly had thrown a little cash her way. After all, if she had that much disposable income and she knew Devon was barely eking by, why wouldn't she share a little with . . . Devon stopped and berated herself for having such avaricious thoughts.

Her only bonus from the case was a budding friendship with James Florio. They got together several times for coffee, saw a couple of movies, and went to the zoo one Saturday afternoon. It was hard for her to determine exactly where things were headed for them, but they never ran out of conversation and as long as they continued to make plans, Devon was happy. James took things at a cautious pace, and although she was more than ready for him to make advances toward her, he maintained his gentlemanly decorum, and she tried to accept it gracefully.

Her clothes were laid out on the bed, ready to be packed. She hadn't been to the beach in a very long time and was looking forward to the change of scenery. That morning she had picked up some brochures at the travel agency along with their airline tickets, and she hoped that the weather would cooperate so that she and Milly could do a little exploring along the Outer Banks. Tomorrow at about noon they would arrive on Roanoke Island and make the short drive to the town of Manteo for the reception. She packed her new dress last in the hope of avoiding as many wrinkles as possible. They had had so much fun shopping the day before. Milly had chosen a conservative navy suit with white trim and pearl buttons. She talked Devon into an elegant red crepe dress that fit her perfectly and accented her slim figure. Devon flushed with guilt now as she remembered that Milly had insisted on paying for their dresses and matching shoes. What made her think she deserved anything more?

The weather at the beach was perfect. Cool air. Sun warm enough for them to leave the windows down on the rental car and take in the salt air. They chatted the entire trip, and although Milly still seemed a little low on energy, she assured Devon the ocean air was just what she needed.

Emily Carson was waiting for them on the wraparound front porch of the LobLolly Inn when they arrived in their rental car. The B & B was so charming and homey that it looked as though it could easily have been her residence. She was a pleasant-looking woman in her mid-to-late fifties, with fine features and dressed in a pastel pink and green flowered dress that draped softly over her tall frame. Her honey-colored hair was perfectly coifed, her hands held gracefully together in front of her, and she stood with perfect posture. As they approached the porch steps she smiled sweetly the way that most well-bred southern women were once taught to do.

"Welcome, ladies. It's a pleasure to meet you both. We are so very honored that you were able to make the trip. Everyone is looking forward to meeting you this evening." She had the most melodic southern accent Devon had ever heard.

"Thank you, we're delighted to be here," Milly said appropriately.

"I'll show you to your rooms. I'm sure you'd like to get settled in and rest a bit before this evening's activities. Now, if you need any little thing at all, you just let me know and I'll see to it."

In the parlor a few guests were playing cards and drinking iced tea. They looked up and greeted Devon and Milly as though they were old acquaintances, inviting them to join the group later on. Another couple was studying travel brochures and didn't even notice them as they walked by. It was wonderful to be away from her everyday life.

Ten, eleven, twelve—a short staircase to the second floor where their rooms were located adjacent to one another. They were spacious rooms with twelve foot ceilings and decorated with floral chintz fabrics and antique furniture. Everything matched. Devon was in heaven. Milly didn't really seem to notice but acted pleased anyway. She was much more impressed with the poetry books on the bookshelf.

Emily chatted a few minutes longer, left directions to the Palmer House on Devon's night table, and then sashayed down the stairs. Milly decided to take a nap while Devon poured over her maps and brochures and made a plan to drive down Route 12 along the

Outer Banks the following day and sightsee all the little towns and beaches.

They arrived at the Palmer House right on time. The room was crowded with smiling faces, and Emily Carson took great pride in introducing them to all the members of the Lighthouse Preservation Society. There was a brief presentation detailing how their donation would be used, and they were each given an engraved miniature lighthouse with their names and the date on it, in addition to a certificate naming them as honorary members of the L.P.S. A sumptuous feast of traditional southern cuisine was served, and while they were finishing their dessert and coffee, a small man with bushy eyebrows and a pinched expression on his face stepped up to the podium. He had to stand on his toes and crane his neck to reach the microphone. He reminded Devon of a baby bird straining to reach its mother's beak for the worm. She covered her mouth with her napkin and laughed. He thanked the society's newest contributors and invited them to check on the restoration progress any time they wished.

The evening turned out to be quite pleasant. Devon had to admit she loved all the attention. Milly, on the other hand, was as gracious as always but downplayed the fuss over the money as much as possible. She was more excited about being at the coast than at being fawned over by well-meaning but somewhat snobbish socialites. By 10:30 only a few members remained in the reception area, and Devon and Milly made their way to the door.

"I had such a nice evening, Mil, but I never realized how exhausting small talk could be," confessed Devon.

"I know what you mean," Milly agreed. "Tomorrow we'll have a relaxing day beach combing and just goofing off."

"Yup. Got it all planned out this afternoon while you were napping," Devon said.

The drive back to the Lob Lolly Inn was quiet, and as they pulled into the parking lot, Devon noticed that Milly had leaned her head against the window and fallen asleep.

"Come on, Mil, wake up. We're back at the hotel." She shook her gently. Poor old girl sure gets worn out easily these days, she thought.

"Oh, right. Guess I dozed off for a minute."

They paused outside their rooms for a moment before turning in. "Let's get an early start tomorrow, huh, Mil? How 'bout rolling out of here at 8:00 A.M. and we'll make our way down the coast toward the cape."

"Whatever you say, luv. You're the driver. See you in the morning."

"G'night." Devon yawned and realized she was a little tired herself, so she decided to follow Milly's lead and get a good night's sleep. Someone had come in while they were gone, turned down the covers on the bed, and left an extra quilt on the chair. The goose-down pillows were plumped up and a chocolate truffle on a miniature doily was placed on top. "I could get used to this," she laughed, pushing her fingers down into the mattress to check it out. Nice and firm. Not like her sagging, lumpy bed at home.

She crawled into bed and wiggled around until she made a warm spot, savoring the luxury of her surroundings, however temporary.

At three o'clock in the morning, Devon jackknifed out of bed in a cold sweat. Her nightgown was soaked with perspiration and clung to her skin. She was shaking uncontrollably and her breathing was sporadic. Her hands groped in the dark for the light. It wasn't there. She was momentarily disoriented and then realized the lamp was on the other side of the bed. She clicked it on and looked around the room. Her suitcase and toiletry bag lay on the floor where she had left them. Still not convinced she was awake, she pinched her thigh so hard a red mark appeared and she winced with pain.

Sitting on the side of the bed she tried to figure out what it meant. The dream was similar to the one she had had a few weeks ago when she fell asleep at her work table. Except tonight it was not a dream — it was a nightmare.

It had the same beginning. Flashes of light. She was in a cold, damp, confined place and was climbing endless stairs. It was urgent that she get to the top. She was running from something or some-one. It was dark, but when the bright light flashed she got glimpses of a winding staircase and a narrow metal railing. She could hear someone close behind her, breathing heavily in pursuit. There were distant cries, but the direction from which they came was undis-cernible. Flashes of light. Her right hand clung to the cold railing while her left dragged along the moist, dimpled surface of a curved wall. She was counting steps. One-hundred-ten, one-hundred-eleven. Out of breath. Still climbing. *Where is this place?* She had left some-thing behind. It was important to her. Very important. *What was it?* Flashes. Two-hundred-one, two . . . How many steps were there? Still being pursued. Two-hundred-twenty. She had to go back and get it. *Get what?* Two-hundred-forty-one, forty-two . . .

The images were out of sequence, jumbled, and confusing. But un-like the dream about Winborne, every visual detail was crystal clear. She remembered that, before climbing the stairs, she had been dig-ging in a small pit. Her shovel caught on a root that began moving and then turned into a rope. A metal ring had been hammered into a cement wall that seemed within a foot of where she was digging. The rope was securely attached to it. She was cold and wet but con-tinued to dig, as if possessed. After digging even deeper, she stopped and pulled hard on the rope. On the other end, as if summoned from its grave, rose a heavy metal box. She jimmied it open and inside the rusted fortune cookie was something beautiful—stacks of one-hundred-dollar silver certificates. Too many to count.

Now she was running in slow motion and then climbing the stairs again. Two-hundred-fifty-three . . . The breathing behind her was a little farther off now but nonetheless threatening. Flashes of light. Two-hundred-sixty-four, two-hundred-sixty. . .

Exhausted, she finally reached the top. The light was flashing above her, circling around. The danger was close again. Very close. She could smell his acrid sweat. Suddenly, a whip of salt air stung her face and she could see the bluish light of a full moon through a doorway in front of her. She crawled on hands and knees through the doorway and onto a narrow platform. Above her head the pulsating beacon of the lighthouse flashed its beam into the night sky, and the frenzied seagulls cried out a warning as they moved up and down in the currents of air, like marionettes. Devon knew she had to escape, but there was only one way down and that was not a feasible option.

She heard him heaving for air and then she saw him. He was within a few feet of her. His bulky frame filled the doorway. Nebulous shadows cast by the rising moon obscured his face, but she could sense his evil intentions. Without warning he pounced, reaching out a muscular arm and circling her throat with his thick fingers.

She twisted and jerked to free herself, but his grip only tightened, and she felt the veins in her neck bulge from the constriction. Her fists pummeled his powerful limbs, but it had not the slightest effect on him. His face was featureless in the shadows, but as he moved forward again, this time to finish her off, he stepped into a sliver of moonlight and she could see a horrifyingly sick smile on his face.

She gasped for air, and as with one last desperate attempt, she opened her mouth to plead for her life . . . she awoke.

$\sim$

*B*reakfast was served in the doily-laden parlor on the first floor of the Inn. Devon was nursing her third cup of coffee by the time Milly joined her at the table.

"You look worse than I feel. Didn't sleep well last night?" Milly asked.

"Morning, Mil. Yeah, you could say that. I tossed and turned all night." Devon was going to tell her about the nightmare but changed her mind. Milly had suffered enough stress over the last few weeks and was finally regaining her vigor. Or, so Devon thought. The last thing she needed was to be burdened by her fretful banter. It was just a bad dream—best to forget about it.

"How about you? Did you sleep okay?" The raccoon circles under Milly's eyes gave Devon her answer.

"I think so. But eight o'clock sure tapped me on the shoulder in a hurry."

"Coffee?" Devon asked.

"Uhmmm."

Devon pressed the last few crumbs of her coffee cake under the tines of her fork and ate them. Try as she might, it seemed impossible to keep her mind from replaying the dream. Not even the home-cooked breakfast in front of her could divert her thoughts for more than a few minutes at a time. All that money. Just waiting there for someone. Imagine the life she could have for herself with even half that much. Everything she ever dreamed of could be at her fingertips. Could it be possible? No, that was crazy. It was just a dream—

probably the result of too much sweet potato pie from the night before.

"Hello? Anybody in there?" Milly teased.

"Oh, sorry. Just daydreaming," Devon said but then almost immediately drifted off in thought again while Milly was ordering her breakfast. But—just what *if* there was money buried out there? Impossible. Even if she decided to pursue this harebrained notion, she had no idea where to start looking. There were so many lighthouses in that area. It could be any one of them and she didn't have the time to research the details. No. This was ludicrous. Besides, there was no way the authorities would let her keep it even if she did find some buried treasure. Unless she didn't turn it in. But that was stealing. Wasn't it?

Somewhere inside she felt a twinge of guilt, immediately overridden by intrigue. Maybe it was worth checking out. After all, her waking dreams had turned out to be pinpoint accurate other times. Was this really that much different? Her thoughts ping-ponged back and forth until at last, she reluctantly decided to ask Milly's opinion about the dream and her notion to try and find the lighthouse.

"Mil, as soon as you're finished eating, we'd better get a move on if we want to get all the way to the Cape today," she began. "Oh, and before we go, there's something I want to ask you about. . ."

"Hold on. There's something I need to tell you first." Milly had a strange expression that Devon had seen before. "I don't think I'll be joining you today. I'm going back home on the 10:00 o'clock flight."

"What? Why?" Devon was stunned.

"I think I'm still fighting that darn flu bug. I guess I never really got rid of it. Don't get that look on your face, Devon," she let out a laugh. "I don't feel that bad, just tired. I'm no spring chicken, you know. Let's make the trip again in the spring and stay four or five days. It would be warmer then and we'd have more time to sight-see."

"We don't have to go anywhere. We can just stay here and walk down to the beach for an hour or so. You know, just take it real easy." Forget the adventure, she thought. It was a dumb idea, anyway. Devon really wanted to enjoy their mini-holiday, and it wouldn't be the same if she were alone. "Mil, are you sure?"

"I'm sure. I've already called from my room and made the arrangements. I'm sorry, Devon, I know you're disappointed. I'll make it up to you. I promise," she said regretfully.

"No, no. It's okay. You don't need to apologize. I just hope you get to feeling better. I should go back with you. I don't feel right about you traveling alone when you're not feeling well."

"For heaven's sake, Devon, it's only one day. Stop fussing. I'll be just fine."

"You'll go back to the doctor, right?"

"Yes, yes, of course, if it will make *you* feel better. Now, what was it you wanted to ask me?"

"Huh? Oh—nothing, it's not important," Devon said.

"All right then, have a good time and I'll see you when you get home. We'll have tea," Milly said reassuringly. She leaned over and they hugged each other.

Devon just hated to see her go.

There was a small souvenir shop on the next block that sold junky gifts, candy, and maps. Devon stopped in to look around. Next to the pecan logs was a shelf of pamphlets and an empty space where a few books on the history of the lighthouses had been. Devon bought a map and helped herself to the free pamphlets. There were three lighthouses within driving distance that she could explore. She decided to drive North to Currituck Beach Lighthouse in Corolla, then head back south, stopping at Bodie Island next and Cape Hatteras last. There was one other lighthouse that was a possibility, but Ocracoke Island was a long drive and ferry ride away, and there was not enough time in one short day to explore all four. With her plan in place, Devon started out. She felt an unmistakable surge of excitement that she could not ignore. And although she was worried about Milly and missed her, she felt rather silly about what she was doing and decided she was glad she was alone. She stopped at the local hardware store to pick up a heavy-duty shovel and put it next to her beach bag on the back seat, along with a couple of packs of Nabs and a diet cola.

It was a beautiful drive to Currituck. The sky was clear and she sang along with the oldies on the radio as she neared her first destination. Because it was off-season and the tourist visiting hours were shortened, the lighthouse was not yet open to the public. Devon walked around the sturdy red-brick lighthouse and tried to recall any clues from the dream that might help her determine whether she was at the right location. Seagulls squawked and sailed effortlessly above her, and the sun warmed her face. The surrounding view was beautiful, but nothing seemed familiar. It didn't feel right. She put her hands on the warm bricks in the hopes that she might "see" something. Nothing happened. But with her eyes closed and her mind focused on the dream, she could remember bits and pieces of the exterior of the lighthouse, and it was definitely not red brick. Black and white. Yes, she recalled its being black and white. She returned to the car and headed South on Route 12 toward Bodie Island. There was no point wasting time in Currituck when there were still two more possibilities waiting for her.

LIBBY'S Diner was crowded with scruffy fishermen and others

whom she guessed to be the "regulars." It being the only eatery within miles, she wasn't too surprised and took a seat at the counter. Soup and a sandwich sounded like a quick lunch order.

Twenty-five minutes later, she was served a bowl of greasy vegetable soup that looked like it had been "ripening" in the pot for weeks and a sandwich with sandpaper for bread and lettuce as limp as a fruit roll-up. The waitress looked surprised when Devon said "no thanks" to the fluorescent cherry pie. It took another ten minutes to get her check. By the time she got back on the road, the sky had lost its brilliant blue and faded to a colorless gray.

It was only five more miles to Bodie Island. Her anticipation heightened at the sight of the black-and-white stripes of the lighthouse in the distance. It wouldn't be long now. Devon parked the car and was surprised to see there were no tourists there. When she walked up to the horizontally striped lighthouse, she could see a sign posted on the door that it was not open to tourists at any time. She was disappointed, but then decided it was actually a bit of luck if this was where she needed to start digging. There was not another person anywhere in sight.

The lighthouse seemed smaller than the one in her dream, and the horizontal black-and-white stripes weren't quite right, either. She scanned her memory. Something else was missing from the picture, too. She sat down on the ground and looked up at the light tower, searching for the answer. Total blank. There was nothing else to be gleaned from this spot. This was not the right lighthouse. Maybe there was no *right* lighthouse. Devon started to think about how absurd her behavior was and decided to go back to the inn. She was getting caught up in her own foolish fantasy. Instead of enjoying the scenery and relaxing, she was traipsing up and down the coast like a landlocked pirate looking for an imaginary chest of gold.

She slid behind the wheel and sat there collecting her thoughts for a moment. Her stomach was rumbling, and she wondered whether there might still be a few muffins in the dining room left over from breakfast. The thought of all those warm, fragrant muffins piled high on doily-covered dishes seemed to ease the disappointment of her aborted adventure. And then, suddenly, she made the connection. The delicate cutwork of the doilies—the elaborate ironwork surrounding the balcony of the lighthouse in her dream. That's what was missing. That was the clue she was looking for. She grabbed the map from the seat beside her and scanned both sides for pictures of the lighthouses. None. There was no time to go looking for another souvenir shop for books. The pamphlets were in a pile next to her purse and she riffled through them until she saw Cape Hatteras Lighthouse—the last one on her list. Her heart was pounding. The picture showed a towering structure with black and white diagonal not horizontal, stripes, and on the inside page was a close-up of the filigree ironwork at the top. Jackpot. This was the right one. It just had to be. She picked up the map again and checked the mileage to Cape Hatteras. There was still enough time to get there before dark and look for the money.

Nothing could stop her now. Nothing, except running out of gas. The red marker on the dash showed less than a quarter of a tank left. Devon would stop at the next station, fill it up, and be on her way without any further delays.

VIII

~

BOBBY

~

1990

The gas station was unusually busy for a November day, and Bobby cursed as he got up out of his soiled chair to help Jimmy, his young employee, pump gas. He was the boss—he shouldn't have to do this anymore. His legs were stiff and his back ached a little. As he brushed past the teenager, he cursed again.

"Don't these people know summer's over? Goddamn, don't anyone stay home anymore?" It never occurred to him that "these people" kept him from the welfare line.

Jimmy was oblivious to his boss's comments and continued to wash the windshield of a station wagon stuffed with beach paraphernalia, two cranky adults, a cocker spaniel, and most important, a fifteen-year-old girl with long blond hair and a face as luscious as a Georgia peach. He must have washed the windshield four times before Bobby came over and slapped him on the back of the head, reminded him that people could wash their own damn windows, and told him to get his ass moving on to the next car.

In less than three years Bobby had squandered all the money that he had stolen from his brother on women, liquor, and gambling. Other than buying himself a color TV, the only worthwhile investment he had made was purchasing the filling station. For several years he was obsessed with trying to figure out where Mack had hidden the rest of the money. As time passed, though, alcohol and his own lack of initiative lulled Bobby back into his old familiar way of life. He convinced himself that it was unlikely there was more money, anyway. Mack was just trying to impress him. He didn't have the brains to pull something like that off. Not without Bobby finding out. And besides, how much more could there have been? Eventually, his pursuit of the money was forgotten.

The station brought in just enough for him to get by without having to work anywhere else. As long as he could afford a regular six-pack and a periodic bottle of J.D. Black Label whiskey, he was satisfied. He never married. Why tie yourself down to someone who'd cheat on you in the end? Women were nothing but a headache and not worth the trouble.

Two more cars pulled in for gas. "What the hell is going on around here?" he said to Jimmy. "Is it a freakin' holiday or somethin'?"

This time Jimmy heard him and answered. "I guess you ain't read the paper today. Some do-gooders come down here yesterday to get some kind of award. Accordin' to the paper, they donated some money to fix up that old lighthouse down the way. Guess some people are volunteering to clean up and such. Seems like there's better ways to spend your money, huh, boss?"

"Damn right, Jimmy." Bobby grumbled and went back to the office and picked up the paper. He was only mildly interested in the article and glanced it over just to see how much money was being spent. The two women in the picture looked like typical "rich bitches" to him. All dressed up in fancy clothes and smiling like they were something special. The younger one was a looker, but the older broad was so short, he thought she looked as though she were sawed off at the knees. He threw the paper in the trash can and popped open a brew. The kid could handle the rest of the customers—he was through working for the day.

At 6:00 P.M. Jimmy went home, and Bobby was about to close the station for the day when a car pulled up. He started to wave the woman off and tell her the pumps were locked when he thought he recognized her, from where he wasn't sure. He seldom ventured outside Buxton and had few repeat customers. If the remoteness of the area didn't keep them away, then his irascible nature and bad service

THE FACE FINDER   **157**

did. Even the locals avoided him. Most customers were just passing through on their way to the more popular tourist areas.

He walked over to the car and stared at the young woman. Where had he seen her?

"Hi. Can I get some gas?" she asked in a friendly tone.

"Well, I ain't sellin' bunny rabbits, girlie. How much you want?" He was sure he had seen her before.

"Fill it up, please." What a jerk, she thought. Bobby circled around the car and put the nozzle in the tank. He never took his eyes off her. The pump clicked off.

"That'll be fifteen dollars even. I seen you before . . . you from around here?"

"No." She handed him a twenty-dollar bill and then apologized. "Sorry, I don't have anything smaller."

"Christ-a'mighty—hold on. I gotta go to the office and get change." He pushed open the greasy office door and fumbled in the register for a five-dollar bill. When he came back around the counter he kicked the trash can and the newspaper fell out onto the floor. He picked it up and there she was. Front page. Same girl.

"Goddamn, maybe the little bitch will give me some of that money she loves to throw away." He shoved the five-dollar bill in his pocket and walked toward her. He leaned over the window and scanned the inside of the car with his bloodshot eyes. The rental car smelled clean, and on the back seat were mostly girlie items except for one thing that seemed out of place. The heavy-duty shovel caught his eye.

"Clam diggin'?"

"Huh . . . what?" she said. He was so close she could smell the alcohol on his breath. Devon really wished Milly hadn't gone home.

"You goin' clam diggin' with that shovel?"

"No, I . . . uh, well, maybe," she stammered.

"Well, what are you goin' diggin' for then?" He enjoyed making her squirm. He loved to taunt and prey on anyone whom he could intimidate; she was easy. Even easier than Mack had been.

"Look, I just want to get on my way to Hatteras Lighthouse before it closes. So if you'll just give me my change, I'll be out of your way." Devon tried to stay cool.

"Don't have no change, miss," he smiled.

"What?" Devon asked.

"I *said*, I don't have no change. No fives, no ones, no change. Comprende? Unless you wanna give back the gas, I'd guess I just got me a five-dollar tip."

"Yeah—okay, fine. Keep the change."

She started to close the window and get out of there as fast as she could, but he put his hands on the door, leaned in even closer, and whispered in her ear.

"Are you sure you don't need nothin' else? Maybe your hot little engine needs some service, huh?"

The hairs on the back of her neck stood at attention. She jammed on the gas pedal and sped out of the station. She could hardly breathe, she was so frightened.

Bobby could hardly breathe either—he was laughing so hard.

He wiped the beer from the corners of his mouth. "I bet I gave her somethin' to think about tonight," he said, still laughing as he started to lock up the office. He had set the newspaper on the counter, and now he picked it up and looked at the picture again. For some reason he decided to read the entire article about the two women from the city. Milly was described as the heir of a wealthy businessman from Asheville named Edmon Winborne who had disappeared some forty years ago and left all his money to her. Devon, the young woman pictured next to her, was her companion and helped identify the missing uncle by some weird process he'd never heard of. He opened another beer and tried to understand. She put the face back on the stiff and the cops figured out who he was and now she was some kind of celebrity. Bobby kept reading.

The older woman was grateful and made a huge donation for lighthouse restoration in the girl's name. Big deal. If he had that much money he sure as hell wouldn't be giving it away—he'd close down that damn station and retire. He looked at the paper and laughed one more time about how bad he scared that little bitch. She was better lookin' than the picture in the paper, though. Probably a teaser. He hated those kind. Showed it off but wouldn't give it up. Bobby started thinking about how long it had been since he was with a woman. Too long. "Maybe she'd like a little company to-night?" he rasped. He wasn't ready to go back to his trailer, not just yet. Hatteras was only a few miles away, and he had no intention of letting that little filly get away.

As he drove down the bumpy two-lane road, he went over the ar-ticle several times in his mind. A millionaire from Asheville who died forty years ago. He thought about the last time he saw Mack and how he went on and on about that stupid summer job up in the mountains. Was it Asheville or Nashville? And about the rich boss that gave him the bonus. He was fairly sure that his brother's visit had been about the same time that this guy in the paper disappeared. Mack had told him his name, but he couldn't recall it. For the first time Bobby cursed the alcohol that now dimmed his memory.

Finally, he started to fit the pieces together, but it seemed too good to be true. If it was the same man, then maybe Mack *had* been telling the truth. Except that it wasn't any bonus—he had stolen the money. It was coming together now. The rich guy's disappearance, Mack's hidden money, the girl finding out who the old man was, the shovel on her back seat. She must have somehow found out where the rest of Mack's stash was. If she had, Bobby could be rich again. He pushed the gas pedal harder. All he had to do was follow her and wait until she dug it up and then he would claim what was rightfully his. However much it was.

He would take the money, scare her real good to keep her quiet— threaten her if he had to. Bobby knew she would be smart enough not to squeal on him. If she did, she would be just as guilty of stealing the money as him. Besides, she was too much of a goody-two-shoes to take a chance like that.

Twice in a lifetime a fortune was going to fall in his lap, and this time nothing was going to get in his way. He parked his car a little way down the road and walked behind the dunes toward the lighthouse. He moved in as close as possible and perched behind a tree, motionless, like an animal fixed on its prey and waiting for the kill. His watch tracking her every move.

When the last of the tourists filed into their cars to go home, Devon got out of hers and looked around. It appeared she was alone. Above her the colorless sky had given way to stacks of ominous thunderheads in the early afternoon, and now the wind had begun to gust. There was a strange feeling in the air, but she assumed it was the impending storm.

She walked over to the lighthouse, counted the granite side panels along the foundation wall, and stopped in front of the fourth one.

Her fingers traced a jagged crack that ran down the side of it. The sharp edge made it clear it was real and not just wishful thinking. In her dream there had been a crack in the panel that marked the spot where the money was buried. She looked around and when she was alone, she began digging.

Bobby couldn't believe his eyes or his luck. The money had been buried there all these years right under his nose. He never even thought to poke around the lighthouse. Made sense, though. Mack, the sentimental fool, would pick some place like that where they played as kids. Probably conjured up some sappy memory of a family and figured it to be the perfect spot.

He watched as she dug furiously, and it amused him that she was doing all the work for him. Then she stopped and put the shovel down. The daylight was almost gone, and it was hard for him to see what she was tugging at. He started to move out from behind the tree to get a closer look, when his foot caught on a surface root and he fell. An animal-like groan escaped from his lungs as his bulky frame hit the ground.

Devon whirled around and their eyes met. She froze. He charged. The adrenaline surged through her body like a rip tide, and she leaped out of the hole where she had been digging and ran. She had to think fast. Not many choices. The ocean—she would drown. The road—he would catch her in no time. On the other side of the lighthouse was a dense pine forest. If she could get there quickly enough, there might be a chance for her to hide.

A light mist began to fall, and Devon saw with dismay that the edge of the trees was farther than she had estimated. She fell back on the decrepit door of the lighthouse to catch her breath and it creaked open. The hinges were rusted and loose, and the door could no longer be locked because of its misalignment. Without hesitation she removed one of her loafers, tossed it in the direction of the woods, and then slipped inside the lighthouse. If she was lucky, the man from the gas station would see the decoy and continue running toward the trees. Devon looked around as best she could in the dark and discovered there was nowhere to go but up. Maybe there was a room at the top, a small cubby hole, anything, that she could hide in. She started climbing the stairs. No need to count this time. She knew the exact number from her dream. On the second tier she heard a noise echo up the stairwell from below. She knew what that was, too. He had followed her into the lighthouse.

The game had begun.

As Devon climbed step after step, tier after tier, her feelings began to churn inside her. She was becoming less afraid and more angry. *Who was he, anyway?* What gave him the right to scare her away? She was sick and tired of being the one who always gave in. It was her money, her future, her freedom. She had found it, and she was not going to leave it behind for him. Not for anyone. Her determination mechanically lifted her legs up the steps. This was a chance for her to have a new life. And she was going to take it—at all costs.

At the top, and out of breath, she paused for a moment to listen. He was not far behind. She could smell him. Alcohol, cigarettes, and sweat mingled together. A nauseating meld that attempted to suffocate her. She had to find a way to get out of there. Even though it was dark, there was no place to hide.

The seagulls were beckoning her out onto the watchtower balcony. It was slick from the moist night air, and the light mist that had now turned into a gentle rain. Now she knew why she had crawled on her hands and knees in the dream. Devon crawled to the side opposite the doorway, standing up and waiting with her back against the wall. She had no idea what to do next. No escape except over the edge. Panic started to wash over her as she remembered the sensations of falling from her recent dreams. She had been wrong; the premonition wasn't about Winborne falling down the steps after all, but rather, about herself. She felt nauseated. It was hopeless.

And then he was standing there in front of her. The light from the beacon flashed across his face to reveal a sinister smile. Rain trickled down his neck, and his chest was moving up and down with his rapid breathing. She slid an inch or so to the right along the wall.

"That money belongs to me, missy. I should of had it a long time ago and I ain't waitin' another minute longer for it. Mack willed it to me." His speech was slurred but he continued, "That Winborne fella gave my brother the money for savin' his life. Tell me somethin,' sweet thing. How in hell did you know where to find it?"

Devon moved again, a little further this time. She said nothing.

"I asked you a question, girlie. Don't you have no manners?" He took a step closer. She could see his pant leg was torn and dragging along the floor of the watchtower.

"I . . . had a dream," she stammered buying for time.

"What'd you say?" He moved closer again.

"I said, I saw it all in a dream. The lighthouse, the steps, the money . . . everything." *Did he say something about Winborne?* It was hard to think straight. She knew he was going to push her over the side and make it look like an accident. Why didn't he just get it over with already? Because, she realized, he was enjoying himself.

"Liar. Mack left that pint-sized friend of yours a letter or somethin' tellin you where he buried the money. Well, it don't matter anyhow 'cause I ain't givin' you the chance to give it away a second time."

"Mack?" she whispered. She had no idea who he was talking about. Unless Mack was the young man who carried Winborne's body out of the manor house. Could he and this man really have been brothers?

He had stopped smiling now, and his icy glare rendered Devon motionless. It was over. The lighthouse dream had stopped before she could see how it ended, but her gut was telling her that this was the final scene.

Bobby lunged forward with his arm outstretched to grab her. She could see the thick fingers reaching for her neck. Instinctively, she jerked to one side. His torn pant leg caught on a protruding nail and he stumbled forward and fell. He landed hard and slid a few feet until he stopped beneath a section of the broken railing, inches from the edge of the platform. He cursed and grabbed at her, but she had moved well out of the way. Bobby looked up at her with a venomous expression and started to get back to his feet. He began to laugh as he pulled his rain-soaked body upright with noticeable difficulty. He was much older than the last time he had been on the watch tower. And then, unexpectedly, he slipped a second time on the rain-slick surface and careened backward through the gap in the railing and over the side. One hand clung to the platform floor in a futile attempt to save his life, the sharp edge cutting into his flesh. Devon, as stiff as a pillar of stone, was unable to so much as blink. The lighthouse beacon flashed, and she watched in slow motion as the weight of his dangling body pulled his fingers from their desperate clutch. When the light flashed again, all that was left was a small pool of blood.

Her body felt numb and her mind was churning in a vacuous

state of confusion. It was as though someone else were in control of her movements. She was aware that she was moving away from the platform and back down the dark winding staircase. Once outside the lighthouse door again, the stinging rain snapped her back to the immediate reality of her situation. She would not allow herself to visualize his horrific end. Instead, she kept focused on her reason for being there in the first place. The money. It began to pour even harder, and although Devon was chilled to the bone, she went back to the pit and retrieved the metal box. The sand was already beginning to fill in the hole and the ocean would wash over it as soon as the storm hit land. Maybe the encroaching waves would wash his body out to sea, too, taking with it the secrets of that horrible night.

Her bare foot was hot and throbbing from sand spurs that were ground into her tender skin when she raced up the stairs and then pushed further in when she came back down. It was a painful reminder to retrieve the shoe she had tossed aside earlier.

The low hanging storm clouds made the night impossibly black. She guessed her way back to the right spot, got down on her hands and knees, and groped in the darkness in all directions until finally her hands touched upon the soggy leather loafer. She never saw the broken body that lay only a few more inches to the right and could easily have met her reach.

On her way back to the hotel she passed the filling station. Some impulse she didn't understand made her suddenly pull the car into the driveway. The whole day had been so bizarre—but seeing the station under the dim street lamp confirmed that everything had, in fact, been real. She had never even come close to having her life threatened before, and it came as quite a surprise how powerful her survival instincts were. A new confidence was born in her that changed her. For that she was grateful.

She parked the car in front of the office, got out and peered through the greasy fingerprinted windows. Inside it was dimly lit with one bare bulb and revealed nothing more than the repugnant debris of Bobby's slovenly existence. Devon walked around to the back of her car, opened the trunk, and took out the shovel. She wiped the handle clean of sand and fingerprints and then positioned it upright against the office door. It was a farewell to the man who had almost stolen her life—and her fortune. A tombstone of sorts. She paused for a moment and was taken aback when she saw her reflection in the glass and realized there was an almost undetectable, peculiar, smile on her face.

IX

~

DEVON

~

1990

$\mathcal{T}$he drive back to the LobLolly Inn was a blur. However, Devon was careful not to exceed the speed limit. The last thing she needed was to be pulled over by a bored beach patrol officer. She was anxious to count the money, but that would have to wait until she felt absolutely safe. This unfamiliar person inside of her was calm and in control, and with little difficulty, she was able to shove the gruesome events of the evening into the recesses of her consciousness and contemplate instead the prospects of what her new-found fortune could do for her. She hardly recognized herself. All she could think about were piles of one-hundred-dollar bills. Bobby was a horrible nightmare that disappeared into the darkness of the night. Her good fortune was all that mattered to her now.

By the time she arrived back at the inn the porch lights were off, and it appeared most of the guests had already gone to bed. It would be easy to slip into the hotel and up to her room without any fuss. She decided to leave the money in the trunk until morning. Safer that way. Her plan to dispose of the metal box was already thought out. She had never realized how good she was at planning.

Devon locked the car and then checked it twice to be sure. Her bare foot landed in a cold puddle of rain water, and she lingered for just a moment to soothe the pain from the sand spurs. Tomorrow she would wear her running shoes. They were roomier and would accommodate her swollen foot. The rain was still coming down hard and dripped off her face and hands. She felt cleansed.

A soft glow filtered through the lace curtains in the parlor windows. Maybe she would buy herself a lovely old home like this when she got back. The foyer was dimly lit with a faux candlestick. She limped up the steps along the side close to the railing where the boards didn't creak. The small puddles of water left by her footsteps were not worth worrying about. They would dry by morning.

After a hot shower, Devon packed her clothes back into her small weekender-sized suitcase. She checked her airline ticket and wrote a brief note thanking Emily Carson for her hospitality and placed it on the bed table. Everything must appear to be in order. It wouldn't be necessary for her to check out of the hotel in the morning, since she and Milly were guests of the L.P.S. and Emily Carson was taking care of the bill.

With everything seemingly accounted for, Devon turned down the chintz comforter and got into bed. Her head sank into the pillow and she lay staring up at the ceiling for a long while. The only thing that unnerved her was her composure. Two days ago, she would have been crawling out of her skin, babbling a stream of plea bargain prayers, and turning inside out with guilt.

Gradually exhaustion began to diminish the adrenaline high she was on, and she closed her eyes. Her breathing was steady and rhythmic. There were no dreams. Just sleep. Heavy, impenetrable sleep.

At 5:45 A.M. her travel alarm went off. The muscles in her legs burned and ached from the rigorous lighthouse climb, and her foot screamed a searing pain as she put her weight on it to stand up. She dressed quickly and straightened the bedcovers out of habit. Her suitcase was ready and waiting by the door. She took one last look around the room and then quietly slipped out. The inn was as peaceful as it had been the night before. All the guests were still sleeping and, Devon supposed, dreaming about the heavenly assortment of muffins and biscuits that would be waiting for them in the parlor when they awoke. For the first time, she thought of Milly and the cozy breakfast they had shared the day before. Her face felt hot, and she pushed the thought aside before she was forced to deal with her feelings. Not now. Denial could be very useful, indeed.

The sun was still contemplating dawn and had not yet broken its first light. Outside the morning air was fresh and sweet, and the stars shone through a clear sky. All evidence of the previous night's storm was erased. It was a new day. A new life. And all too soon, new decisions.

She started to unlock the trunk and hesitated for a moment. Insidious doubts began to filter through the cracks of Devon's new-found strength as subtly as the ambient light of sunrise suffused the sky.

"I won't give in. It's mine," she said and jerked open the trunk. The metal box was in its place. It looked larger than it had the night before. She ran her fingers across the rough eroded surface to be sure it was real. The rust left a dirty orange stain on her fingertips.

She wedged her suitcase in next to it, touched it one more time, and then closed the trunk. A quick look around verified that she had not been seen.

"Just get out of here and get back home. Everything will be okay," she reassured herself. But something was different this morning. Maybe that brief memory of Milly triggered her conscience to step in and challenge her motives. It was getting harder and harder to convince herself that everything <u>was</u> okay. She could feel herself slowly sliding back toward the self with a conscience. The old Devon. The one she knew. Or maybe she was just losing her nerve.

"Don't fall apart now," she said aloud. "You deserve this." There were really only two options. One, she could call the police and tell them about Bobby and the money—and they would never believe her. There was no way to prove that the money belonged to the Win-borne heirs, and even more important no legal justification for her to claim it. She couldn't very well tell them it was hers because she saw it in a dream. They would arrest her and possibly charge her with murder, or grand larceny or submit her to a rigorous psychological evaluation. Her life would be over. Or, two, she could snap out of it, continue with her plan, and get back home and have the life she dreamed of.

The road was virtually devoid of any traffic. A few miles down she spotted a scenic pull-over and decided it was a good place to transfer the money to her travel bag and discard the box. She drove up to the small parking area and looked around. As Devon brushed the hair from her face, she noticed that her hand was trembling. She wondered why. No one had seen her. She hadn't done anything wrong. It wasn't her fault that he fell from the balcony.

Besides, if she hadn't taken the money someone else would have when they started the lighthouse restoration. Emily Carson mentioned that the first thing to be done was to dig around the lighthouse base and reinforce the foundation. Some unsuspecting volunteer would have found the box and would no doubt have given the money to the L.P.S. or some other charity. Or worse yet, kept it for himself. No, the money was hers. She told herself that over and over again. But somehow, each time she did the voice seemed a little weaker and that new Devon a little harder to reach. The only person staring back at her in the rearview mirror now was a guilt-ridden, self-doubting Catholic schoolgirl. Stop it. Stop worrying. Just do what you have to do.

In the parking area was a weather-worn picnic table with a large barrel used as a trash receptacle placed alongside it. Both were anchored down with chains more to defy coastal winds and violent storms than as a deterent to theft. Devon pulled the car up close to the barrel and parked. She left the engine running.

The sun was beginning to paint brilliant shades of yellow, orange, and even red on the tufts of clouds above the horizon. Had it been any other day, she would have enjoyed the splendor of the sunrise and marveled at the intensity of the colors that only nature can produce. But today the sunrise meant only that each degree of increased light brought with it a greater chance of her being seen.

Devon got out of the car and unlocked the trunk. She opened her suitcase and pushed the clothes to one side to make room for the money. In the process, the red dress that she had so carefully packed two days earlier was smashed and crumpled into the corner. Another twinge of guilt and a flash of Milly telling her how lovely she looked in the dress.

The metal box opened easily, and inside the stacks of bills awaited their destiny. There was so much more than Devon had realized. She gathered the bundles two and three at a time and began stuffing them into the suitcase.

Because it was such a short trip, she had chosen her smallest travel bag, which was more than adequate for a few days. But it was apparent that it was not adequate to accommodate weekend apparel plus what she guessed to be about $50,000. She pushed the clothes tighter and tighter into the corners of the suitcase, but it was no use. There was not enough room for all of it. How ironic that her biggest problem now was too <u>much</u> money. Leaving some of the money behind was out of the question. However, leaving her clothes behind was not. She could always get a new red dress.

The sun was almost halfway up and quickly leaving the horizon behind. It was going to be a beautiful sunny day at the beach. An old pickup truck with three men in the cab and several fishing poles and other gear clanging around in the back drove by but the occupants didn't seem to notice her. There would probably be more. She clawed at her clothes until they were all out of the suitcase and scattered about the trunk. The metal box with its seductive bounty was still half full. She picked it up and turned it upside-down, spilling the remaining bundles of money into the suitcase. As it swung open something caught her eye. A water-stained but otherwise intact plain white envelope was stuck to the last bundle. Probably just a tally of how much money.

She peeled it free and shoved it in her pocket and then forced the suitcase shut. Fumbling with her key ring, she found the smallest key and inserted it into the openings, turned it until it clicked, and then pulled up on the latches to be sure the bag was locked. Check. Then she collected the scattered clothes and wadded them into a ball. She placed them on top of the red dress and tied a knot around the whole bundle so that it resembled a knapsack. Next she yanked the metal box out from the trunk and carried it over to the trash barrel. The container smelled foul but was mostly empty, with only a few soda cans and miscellaneous bits of trash in the bottom.

Devon lifted the box over the side of the barrel. It made a loud crash as it hit the bottom of the barrel. She wasted not another second, but ran back to the car and drove away. A chill ran up her spine; she was shivering, and she could taste the salty dew of perspiration on her upper lip. Once on the road, she felt a little safer and tried to regain her composure.

It was hard to keep her mind from wandering, projecting images of Milly's eyes, her parents' loving faces . . . She could almost hear James's laughter, almost feel the warmth of his touch.

Last night it had all seemed so simple. A new life, riches beyond her wildest dreams—no more worries—freedom. Was it really worth losing everyone she loved for money? It was ridiculous to think she could just show up from a two-day trip to the coast with a bag full of money, totally change her way of life, and not have anyone ask any questions. She was such a fool. But regardless of what she thought now, she still had to deal with the situation at hand. She had to follow through. It was almost over.

Just past the stoplight, she spotted the golden arches of McDonald's. She pulled in for a cup of coffee and sat there in the parking lot trying to think of some plausible explanation she could offer up when she got back home regarding her unexpected payload. Nothing came to mind. Devon sipped the last few drops of coffee and pulled around to the trash can to toss the cup in. As she did this she saw a sanitation truck pull into the parking lot and go around to the back of the building. The driver positioned the rigid metal arms of the truck onto the sides of a green dumpster. A moment later the truck groaned and then lifted the container up and over the cab to dump its contents into the back of the truck; there to be crushed. When the dumpster was set back down, the doors on the top of it were folded back and exposed a gaping hole.

Devon immediately spun the car around and headed for the dumpster. This was her break. The choice of which bundle she decided to dispose of would dictate the course of her life. She could toss the clothes or the money. It was up to her.

It only took her a few seconds to retrieve it from the trunk and place it on her lap. She made her decision. By the time anyone found it she would be long gone. No loose ends. Home free.

With her window rolled down, she got as close to the side of the dumpster as possible, grabbed the red bundle of clothing, heaved it into the air, and watched it sail into the mouth of the green giant. It was time to go home.

"You're in 12A, miss," the flight attendant said as she directed Devon to her seat.

"Thanks."

"Would you like some help getting your bag in the overhead compartment?"

"Oh, no . . . no. I can handle it. Thanks anyway." She gripped the handle on the suitcase a little tighter and scanned the attendant's face for signs of suspicion.

The suitcase barely fit into the compartment, but a push here and a shove there and it was finally in. She had assumed it was no larger than the average carry-on bag most people traveled with. If she hadn't been so worried about letting it out of her hands, she could have checked it as she did on the flight down.

Once in her seat Devon took a deep breath and tried to relax. Everything would be all right now. The only other person who knew about the money was gone. She wondered how far he had drifted out to sea and whether he was bobbing up and down in the waves like a buoy. Or if his body was pulled under during the storm by a surging rip tide and was resting on the ocean floor like a sea snake. Either way he was "gone." She preferred that word to "dead."

She closed her eyes and tried to sleep. Although Devon was in a small way proud of herself for escaping Bobby's attempt on her life and maneuvering her way out of town with a suitcase full of cash, in her heart she was deeply ashamed.

Mack had stolen the money from the Winborne family forty years ago, and now she was stealing it from them again. From Milly. If it belonged to anyone, it belonged to Milly. The formidable walls that Devon had built to get herself through her ordeal were beginning to crumble in the face of undeniable truth. She felt a warm stream of tears trickle down her cheeks. She tried to act casual and brush them away, but there were too many. Again, she thought of Milly. Dear Milly. The person in her life whom she cherished the most. It was inconceivable that she actually considered keeping the Winborne fortune. She cradled her face in her hands, pressed her elbows onto her lap and, finally, gave in to her emotions.

By the time the plane began its descent and prepared for landing, Devon had stopped crying and decided to tell Milly the truth. The whole story. No money was worth the pain of losing her dearest friend.

The man next to her smiled at her sympathetically and told her that his wife cried every time he had to go out of town, too. Devon let out a small laugh at the complete idiocy of his observation.

It seemed as though she had been gone for so long. In a certain sense, she had. But now, with her mind made up and her conscience clear, Devon was at peace with herself. For the first time in her life she accepted herself, flaws and all. She realized that courage and strength need not be reserved for perilous situations. Both virtues could be drawn upon in simply choosing to do what was honest. What was right.

It wouldn't be easy telling Milly the truth, but they would talk it all out over tea and somehow come to an understanding. Tomorrow she would crank up the old Chevy and get back in the groove at the museum. And she was going to tell James how she felt about him, too. No more disguises. From now on she was going to say what she meant and deal with her feelings openly.

She reached in her pocket to search for a tissue. Her hankie was soaked with tears, and she wanted to wipe the smeared mascara from her face. Her fingers touched the envelope she had shoved into her pocket at the picnic site. She pulled it out and stared at it for a minute, not sure whether to open it. But not even five minutes ear-

lier she had vowed to deal with things head on, and she guessed this
was the appropriate time to take her first step in that direction. The
envelope had long ago lost its glue, making it easy to remove the
contents. She expected to see a tally of how much money was stored
in the box, and since she had not yet counted it, the thought of that
alone was daunting. What she saw, however, was something alto-
gether different. Inside the envelope was a handwritten letter dated
September 1, 1950.

To: The St. Agnes Home for Children
Dear Sister Anne Catherine,

*Please accept on behalf of myself and my family this donation to
the Children's Home. Many years ago I lost my own children to ill-
ness. I find that providing some degree of comfort and possibly making the lives of these unfortunate innocents a little easier brings me
great joy and somehow eases my own grief.*

*I entrust you to utilize this donation as you see fit for the benefit
of the children and ask only one thing in return. That I remain
anonymous under any and all circumstances. My joy comes from
sharing with the children and not from the accolades of others.*

*With my best regards to you and your staff and my deepest re-
spect for your devotion to the Children's Home, I remain,*

Most sincerely yours,
Edmon James Winborne

Devon was stunned. She wondered whether Milly or anyone else
in the family ever knew about Edmon's donations. Now she understood where Milly's philanthropic nature and nonchalance about
money came from. It was hereditary.

The plane touched down and taxied over to the terminal. Devon
reached up and pulled the cash-laden suitcase from the overhead

compartment. It seemed lighter. She sighed and resigned herself to the fact that the matching bedroom ensemble would have to wait for some other year. And in spite of the fact that she was nervous about what she had to do, she felt relieved and was anxious to see Milly. The sooner she cleared all this up and got back to her normal life the better.

The taxi dropped her in front of her apartment building and Devon stood there a moment before going in. Milly was probably sipping tea and listening to music in her favorite chair, expecting Devon to knock on her door at any moment.

~

CAPE HATTERAS PIER

A small crowd had gathered at the end of the pier. There was a hum of excitement, and even the employees who worked at Bo's Bait Shop had wandered out to take a gander. It was well known that some of the area's largest fish were caught right off that pier in the fertile but notoriously treacherous coastal waters of North Carolina. The proof was pinned up on the back wall of Bo's, where a hundred or more photographs showed proud-faced fishermen displaying their catch. And by all indications of the steadily increasing crowd gathered under the noonday sun, yet another "big one" had been brought in today. Bo looked out the salt-crusted screen door that led to the pier and saw a reporter taking notes for the local newspaper. He had better clear a spot on the wall for a new photo.

About a quarter of a mile down the strand, a few Lighthouse Preservation Society volunteers decided to take a break from their work removing litter from the dunes around the lighthouse and walk down to the pier to see what the commotion was. As they approached the crowd, a photographer pushed by and ran up onto the pier as though the President had just arrived. A bulging gray camera bag with broken zippers slipped off his shoulder as he fumbled inside it to find the right lens. He was anxious and sweaty but appeared focused on his assignment. The youngest of the three volunteers, a college student, was immediately caught up in the excitement. He decided to follow the photographer and get a firsthand look. The other two volunteers, both retirees, stayed at the shore end of the pier, content to cool their feet on the weathered, ash-colored planks shaded by Bo's roof, and wait for the gossip to come to them.

"Hey man, can you see what they caught?" a surfer asked the old sun-dried fisherman standing next to him.

"Naww. Can't get close enough. Don't think it's too big though 'cause they ain't 'gonna hoist it up."

The young volunteer moved past the surfer and nudged closer and closer to the photographer until he was literally on his heels. They were still quite a distance from the center of action and continued moving forward, with the photographer ignoring his shadow. A robust, red-faced woman, dressed in a bright orange-and-green flowered sundress that stuck in between the folds of her belly, suddenly turned around and bolted through the crowd, leaving ample room for both of the young men to step closer. There hadn't been this much excitement at the pier all summer. They were almost within viewing range now, and the volunteer thought he caught a glimpse of something but couldn't make out what it was. If they could just move a little more to the right . . .

"Excuse me, please, Press—coming through," said the photographer with affected authority as he parted the onlookers. Several people turned toward the man with the camera and then obediently moved aside. Never missing a beat, the volunteer moved right with him. The closer they got to the prize, the tighter and quieter the crowd became. Perhaps this was some sort of pier etiquette, like the silence around the greens at pro golf tournaments.

With skilled determination the photographer inched his way through the remaining layers of tightly packed people until he was so close to the catch that he was standing almost directly over it. The volunteer eagerly followed and stood next to him, at last able to satisfy his curiosity. It was a decision he would regret.

He could see laid out on the pier a small, lifeless form no larger than twenty-three inches around and maybe eighteen to twenty inches long. All the oldtimers nodded their heads and agreed that there was no way to accurately identify it. The mutilated flesh however, clearly indicated shark attack. The predators must have had a feast.

The camera clicked again and again, shooting as many angles as possible of the hideously detached human leg that lay on the pier, somehow still partially covered with remnants of denim work pants. It was the unimaginable death. Strips of flesh hung off the bone like bloody ribbons. Everything, even the cuff of the pant, was torn.

X

~

MILLY

~

1990

There were only a few pieces of mail in her mailbox. Nothing exciting. When Devon reached the top of the stairs, she realized that she had not counted them again. She pressed her ear to Milly's door, and as she predicted, heard music playing softly. Her first instinct was to knock on the door, but on second thought, she decided to drop off her mail and check her messages first. Being that close to the confessional prompted a knot in the pit of her stomach. She prayed Milly would not be too angry with her.

On the machine, a message from her mother reminded her that Leora's birthday was in two days. There were a couple of hang-ups and a cheery message from James inviting her out that evening if she was up to it.

Devon walked into her bedroom and tossed her purse on the bed. She smiled as she looked at the tattered comforter. Someday. The reflection she saw in her dresser mirror startled her. Dark circles rimmed eyes, in a pale face. The stress of the last several days had definitely left its mark. After she and Milly had their talk, she would take a long nap. She couldn't possibly let James see her looking like this. The cadavers in his lab probably had more color in their cheeks than she did.

Devon scolded herself to quit fooling around and take care of business. No more procrastinating. She moved toward the door, picked up the small suitcase for the last time, and carried it with her to Milly's apartment. This was going to be the hardest thing she had ever done.

The knot in her stomach tightened as she knocked on the door. Tighter than the knot she had tied in her red dress.

"Milly? It's Devon. I'm back. Want some company?" She cringed at her choice of words. As if it were going to be just another chat session.

"The door's open. I've been expecting you," Milly answered in a distant voice as if from another room.

But when Devon entered the cozy living room, she saw Milly in her bathrobe lying on the sofa. Her head rested on a pillow and a thermometer was nearby on the coffee table.

"Still not feeling well? What's up?" Devon asked.

"Don't know yet. Doc Wilber did some blood work, but the tests won't be in for a few days. He said it's nothing serious. Really. Just a tricky strain of virus that's hard to isolate or something. I really don't feel that bad. Just tired. I can deal with that," she stated.

"Are you sure? Anything I can do for you?" Devon was concerned and Milly picked up on it immediately.

"Devon, relax. I'll be fine. You worry too much. Now tell me about your stay at the beach. Did you enjoy the extra day down there? What did I miss out on?"

That was a loaded question if ever she had heard one. Devon looked at Milly stretched out on the sofa and wondered if indeed this was the right time to discuss such a delicate subject.

"Hellooo?" Milly teased.

Devon laughed, relieved to see Milly still had the energy for a sense of humor.

"Well, are you going to keep me hanging or are you going to tell me about the beach?"

"Uhmmm, actually I have quite a bit to tell you. I'm just not sure where to begin. I guess it started that first night at the Lob Lolly Inn when I had a horrible dream. . . ." and Devon proceeded to confess every excruciating detail of her misadventure. When she was finished talking, her mouth was dry and her lips were trembling. Milly never said a word. Devon told her how deeply sorry she was and that she hoped in time Milly would forgive her. She brought the suitcase over to the couch and opened it up. The bundles of money lay haphazardly in the case along with the letter which she showed to Milly. Finally, Milly sat up and opened her mouth to speak.

"Hmmm. Well—thank you for your honesty, Devon. This must have been very difficult for you to tell me. It might actually have been easier for you to just move away and start over." She paused. "But I'm glad you didn't. I would have missed our Sunday teas terribly." Milly gave her a strained smile. "Look, the important thing is that you told me the truth. It was the right choice. It's just money. Nowhere near as valuable to me as our friendship."

Devon was overwhelmed with emotion. Relief, gratitude, admiration, love, and so many other feelings poured over her all at once that she didn't even notice she was crying. It was over. And Milly was still her friend.

"By the way, we all knew about my uncle's donations. He tried to keep it a secret, but in the end he was found out."

"How?"

"After the publicity about my uncle's disappearance, my family started receiving letters and phone calls from complete strangers. Each one connected to a children's hospital or orphanage. When questioned about their association with my uncle, it was revealed that he had generously supported their institutions for a number of years but had requested to remain anonymous for personal reasons. There had always been rumors about his strange habit of suddenly taking trips with little or no warning. After his funeral service we all understood where he went." Milly tugged at her robe and wrapped it a little tighter.

"Unbelievable," Devon said as she got up and moved over to the sofa next to Milly. She grabbed a tissue, wiped her eyes, and put her hand over her friend's. "I'm so glad that this is all straightened out."

"Me, too. Now, be a luv and make us some tea, will you? I can't seem to shake this chill."

"Coming right up. The usual?" Devon asked as she walked into the kitchen.

"The usual," Milly replied in a voice slightly weaker than before.

The good news was that Milly's test results showed no signs of a viral infection. The bad news was that she was suffering from something far worse. She had always been frail as a child, contracting illnesses easily from anyone she was exposed to who was sick. One winter a particularly virulent strain of the flu had plagued her community and naturally she caught it. She was so ill that she was hospitalized and as a result of the infection developed a severe case of rheumatic fever.

Milly had told Devon about the blood tests but had not told her about the string of other tests Dr. Wilber insisted she go through. Most everything checked out in reasonably good shape for a woman in her mid sixties and with her health history. However, the results from the cardiopulmonary tests showed that the valves in Milly's heart had been damaged from the rheumatic fever and were very weak. Not uncommon for someone who had suffered a case as severe as she did. Dr. Wilber told her she had probably been suffering from congestive heart failure for quite a while, but now that she was getting older it had progressed. He explained that the fatigue, shortness of breath, and general malaise were all due to the heart's inability to pump sufficient blood through her body. He prescribed some medications for her and suggested she come back in a month for a follow-up.

Milly had no intention of going back. There was really nothing that could be done for her, other than getting a new heart. And she was in no way interested in putting herself through that. Life had been good to her, and she saw no reason to tamper with her destiny. Whatever her fate, she would accept it. Besides, longevity had never run in her family anyway.

As the months went by, Devon noticed that Milly had less and less energy. When she inquired about the doctor's suggested treatment, Milly told her that she rejected it and just wished to live out her life naturally. Devon had no choice but to accept Milly's decision and respect it. Instead of trying to change her friend's mind, she decided to do as much as she could to make life easier for her. She helped clean her apartment and take care of her plants. Every afternoon she called Milly from work to see if she needed anything. She made extra portions of food and ate dinner with her almost every evening. Occasionally James would join them, and Devon welcomed the pleasant diversion. No one could have looked after Milly as conscientiously as Devon did. Even Mrs. Gardiner remarked to her husband how independent and self-reliant Devon had become.

Milly continued to have good days and bad days. She never complained but gradually spent more time resting and less time doing the things she loved. It was almost unbearable for Devon to watch her beloved friend begin to fade away.

They did, however, faithfully continue their Sunday afternoon teas.

∼

A year later, with Milly's health still in decline, Devon continued her daily routine of fixing an early breakfast for them both before she went off to work. At lunch she called to check on Milly, and then after work she would stop in for a few minutes to drop off her mail and have a glass of wine before preparing dinner. On the weekends Devon and James spent as much time together as possible, and a good portion of their plans included Milly. They would play board games in her apartment if the weather was inclement, and at other times would just sit in the courtyard and enjoy the fresh air.

On a breezy March afternoon, Devon decided to surprise Milly with tickets to <u>The Barber of Seville</u>. She purchased front-row seats for the two o'clock matinee. Milly usually had more energy during the day and would be more likely to stay awake for it. The key to Milly's apartment hung on her key ring permanently now so that she could check on her neighbor whenever it was necessary. Devon raced into her apartment and told Milly the good news.

It had been so long since Milly had attended the opera. She was genuinely excited and asked Devon to help her decide what to wear. The old sparkle was back in her eyes, and she seemed like her old self as she slipped into a forest-green velvet dress. Devon remarked how it brought out the color in her eyes. She should have done this for her friend months ago. Milly was on cloud nine.

Their seats were wonderful, and as the orchestra tuned up, Devon noticed that Milly could not stop smiling. The performers were topnotch, and when the show was over the audience's enthusiasm pulled them back for several curtain calls. It was the best afternoon they had ever spent together. Like old times. The ride home was quiet, and Devon noticed the fatigue on Milly's face despite her contentment.

"This has been the most wonderful day. Thank you, Devon."

"It was. And you are very welcome. You look a little tired, though. We'll have some soup and then a hot bath for you and call it a day, huh?"

"I think that's a good idea. Maybe I'll skip the soup. "

"Whatever you say, Mil."

They decided to sit for a few minutes in the living room and sip a glass of wine. It seemed the perfect end to a perfect day. When they finished, Devon started to help her to the bedroom to change clothes and get ready for her bath, but Milly touched her arm and stopped her.

"Devon, you don't need to stay this evening. I think I'll just sit here a few minutes longer and savor the day. Why don't you call James and have some fun? I can manage on my own tonight. Really." She was very convincing.

"Are you sure? You know I don't mind."

"I'm positive. Just do one thing for me before you leave. Put the "Barber" soundtrack on. I just have to hear it again."

Devon laughed and popped the CD in the player, kissed her friend on the cheek, and told her she would check up on her later. Milly settled into her favorite chair, thanked Devon again for the marvelous time, and waved good-bye to her as she closed the door.

James and Devon climbed the stairs of her apartment building somewhere around 9:45 P.M. He had taken her to a local pub that was featuring an Irish folk music trio and they ate fish n' chips and drank a few beers. Neither of them was very musical but they tried their best to do a jig on the dance floor anyway. They always had such a good time together and that night was no exception. Their relationship had developed as smoothly and naturally as did hers with Milly. She felt so lucky to have two people in her life who loved her just as she was and who were so dear to her heart. She turned the key to her apartment, opened the door, and then turned to James abruptly.

"Oops. I promised Milly I'd look in on her when we got back."

"Do you want me to come with you?"

"Oh no, I'll just be a minute. She's probably already asleep anyway. Why don't you make some coffee, and I'll be there before you can get the ice cream out of the freezer," she said with a warm smile.

The lights were still on in Milly's apartment, but it was quiet. She smelled a hint of jasmine lingering in the air, a fragrance Milly wore only on special occasions. The CD player was still on but the music had stopped. She clicked it off and chuckled at Milly's childlike exuberance to hear more after they got home.

Everything seemed in order and she walked toward the bedroom to peek in on her friend. Today had been such a success, maybe tomorrow or the next day they would go to the park for a little while. It seemed to do wonders for Milly's spirits to get out of the apartment.

She ran her fingers across the top of the sofa as she walked behind it. It was hard to pinpoint why Milly's apartment was always so cozy and inviting. She had loved it from the first day she stepped in for tea. It felt more like home to her than her own place. And it always smelled so good.

When she came around the other side of the sofa, she saw Milly still sitting in her chair, fast asleep. She hadn't even changed out of her green dress. Devon smiled at her affectionately and went over to her side to wake her.

She put her hand on her shoulder and shook her gently.

"Mil, come on, wake up. I'll help you get out of this dress and into bed." She nudged her again. "Milly? C'mon—wake up. Time for bed. . . . Milly?" Devon touched her hand and then tentatively pressed her fingers to the underside of her wrist to check her pulse.

"Oh God, no, please let this be a dream." But it was not. Milly's weakened heart had slowly stopped beating and succumbed to congestive heart failure. She had died quietly and gracefully—just as she did everything else.

Devon knelt down and put her head on Milly's lap and wept. Her heart ached with a pain the likes of which she had never known. It was as if her soul had been torn in half.

After a long while, she felt James put his arms around her and help her up. After about twenty-five minutes, when she had not returned to the apartment, he had suspected something was wrong.

"It's okay, Devon. I'm sure she died very peacefully. There's nothing you could have done for her," he said reassuringly. "I'll take care of the arrangements—don't worry about anything, honey."

They went back to Devon's apartment and sat on her sofa. Neither one of them spoke much, but Devon remained in the safety of James's loving arms until the ambulance arrived. Milly had always told her he was the kind of man she could depend on.

"Oh Mil, how will I ever get along without you?" she whispered and then buried her head in her hands and wondered whether she would ever be able to stop crying.

XI

~

Devon

~

1996

Sunlight was streaming in through the bedroom windows as Devon examined the clothes that were stacked on the brightly colored yellow and lavender floral bedspread. It looked as though she had everything she needed for the trip, and she began to fill her suitcase. Peals of laughter and rambunctious shouts came from the yard below. She walked over to the open window, held back the matching draperies, and called out to the dark-haired little boy who appeared to be the ringleader.

"Andy, it's time to come in now. Dad will be home any minute."

"Awwh—okay, Mom," he answered with some reluctance.

They hadn't really planned to become parents when they did. But now she couldn't imagine her life any other way. Every time she looked at Andy's face, she was amazed at how much love and happiness one skinny little seven-year-old could generate. He was the absolute joy of her life.

A moment later James pulled into the driveway of their spacious old Victorian style home, and she heard him get out of the Jeep. It had taken them over a year to renovate the house and fix it up exactly they way they wanted it. They were married about ten months after Milly's death and bought the house a few months after that.

Devon had been named as the sole beneficiary of Milly's estate, which turned out to be quite substantial. Along with her antique furniture, books, and music collection was a very large sum of money, in addition to the $200,000 Devon had returned to her. She and James used the money to purchase their home, pay off her student loans, fund Leora's college tuition and pay up the mortgage on her parents' bungalow.

She continued her work at the museum for a while, but when

Andy came into the picture, she decided to devote herself to being a full-time mom. Nathan called her from time to time trying to get her to come back to work, but the most she would accept was a freelance project here and there.

She had everything she had always wanted. But it really wasn't the new house or the money or even the long-desired matching bedroom ensemble that brought her happiness. It was James and Andy. All those dreams of fancy clothes and new cars and tons of money became meaningless. Now that she had more money than she could ever have hoped for, it had lost its elusive charm. In fact, much the same as Milly, she found it burdensome. So they agreed to put a portion away for Andy's education and a hefty sum for their future retirement, and the rest they bestowed on charities. One in particular.

It took them awhile to find St. Agnes' Home for Children. But once they did, they made an appointment with the new director and met with her to set up the arrangements for a trust fund in Milly's name. Sister Anne Catherine had died more than ten years ago but the Winborne name was anything but forgotten at St. Agnes'.

 On their way out of the building, they saw one of the nuns leading a group of preschoolers down the hall in single file. She was holding the hand of one little boy and scolding him for telling a fib. He looked so pitiful as tears cut through the dirt on his face and made narrow streaks down his cheeks. Devon asked the director who he was.

"Oh, that's Andy," she said in an exasperated tone. "He has quite an imagination. Has friends that talk to him in his sleep and tell him secrets. Personally, I don't understand the child. He has a bad habit of rearranging the truth to suit his needs, if you know what I mean. A real handful."

"Yes, I think I know what you mean." Devon looked at James and they both smiled.

Less than six months later, formal adoption papers were signed, and Andy became a part of their family. Devon encouraged him to talk about his imaginary friends, and she always made time to listen. After a few months he settled down and acted like any other kid his age.

"Hey, Dev, you ready to go? Can you believe the weather? It's going to be fantastic camping this weekend!" James hollered up the stairs. Ten to be exact. She had stopped counting steps for the most part, but every once in a while she couldn't help herself.

"Yes, sir." But by the time she answered, he and Andy were already in the bedroom gathering up her suitcase and the fishing gear that had been laid out the night before.

"What about your stuff, James?" she asked.

"Hah! Packed the jeep last night after you went to bed. You can't compete with a pro like me," he joked. But actually, it was true. Until Devon met James, her idea of conquering the great outdoors was mowing her father's postage-stamp-sized lawn. Now hiking, camping, and fishing were a regular part of their lives and she loved it. They would take off for the mountains and find remote areas where they would see as few people as possible. Andy loved the adventure, and James always made sure there was a fishing spot somewhere nearby so that he and Andy could use their new fishing poles.

Today they were going to explore a little farther north than they had ever gone before. New territory. James was keeping it a surprise. Andy was ecstatic.

They packed the car and started on their way. James and Andy sang the theme song from "Davey Crockett" and wore fake raccoon-tail hats. It had become their departure tradition; changing them from city folk to mountain men. Andy had no idea who Davey

Crockett was, but anyone who could kill a "bar" when he was only three, was definitely cool. Devon just laughed and enjoyed the fun of it all. As far as she was concerned, her life was perfect.

They were already at the end of their street corner when the phone rang in her kitchen. On the fourth ring, the machine picked up and recorded the caller's message.

"Hello, Devon. This is Detective Whyte. Well, I guess it's been a while, hasn't it? We have some urgent business to discuss with you, and it's important that you get back to me as soon as possible. I have some questions that I think only you can answer. You know where I can be reached. Call me."

The End

ABOUT THE AUTHOR

Carol F. Fantelli was born in Cleveland, Ohio in 1952, and moved to Raleigh, North Carolina in 1974. She attended Ohio State University for two years and received her bachelor's degree in art from Meredith College in Raleigh in 1977. She has been married for the past 13 years to award winning film and location photographer Steve Murray and lives in Raleigh with her husband and son, Nathan Motylinski.